Blair Atholl's Railway

Howard Geddes

A typically bustling day 17 September 1954 around lunchtime: the morning Glasgow-Inverness passenger train headed by Black 5 No.45357 is leaving helped by an almost new BR Standard 3MT No.77008 assisting from the rear; Black 5 No.44960 with a Perth-Inverness goods train waits in the lay-by sidings, whilst another pilot engine 3MT No.77009 is ready to help it up The Hill. The engine outside the shed is 1916 built ex-Caledonian 4-4-0 No.54476, ready for the local passenger train to Perth. (Harold Bowtell/HRS collection)

On 17 September 1954 an ex-Caledonian 4-4-0 No.54467 heads the two coach 1.30pm local train to Perth; Black 5 No.45389 heads the 12.15pm Perth-Inverness. The tanks may be for drinking water which still needed to be supplied to various remote railway houses. (Harold Bowtell/HRS collection)

© Howard Geddes 2013
ISBN: 978 0 95454858 2

All rights reserved. No part of this publication may be reproduced, stored in a retrieval system or transmitted, in any form or by any means, electronic, mechanical, photocopying, recording or otherwise, without the prior written permission of the publisher.

Published by the Highland Railway Society : www.hrsoc.org.uk.

Printed by Berforts Information Press, Eynsham, Oxfordshire, OX29 4JB

Front cover: The main Station Building in Highland Railway days - note the low platforms and the decorative filigree on the eaves of the chalet-style main block. The Station Master lived on the upper floor. The Duke of Atholl had his own Waiting Room in the farther wing. (Author's collection)

Inset: 6th Duke of Atholl (Blair Castle Archives)

Inside front cover: Representations of the diagrams in Blair Atholl's Signal Boxes when there was one at each end of the station, showing the arrangements for controlling the points and signals, dating from about 1932 when the station layout was fully developed.

For the technically minded, Key Token was in use from the South box to Killiecrankie, Tyer's 2-position block from the North box to Struan and Bell working between the two boxes. In addition, there was an Annett's Key on lever 20 in the North Box which, when extracted, locked signal 20, the Advanced Starter, at danger. Drivers in possession of the Key could pass the signal at danger to Black Island platform, then return to Blair Atholl on the same track. (Author's collection)

Contents

Blair Atholl's Railway

Before the Railway 5
The Coming Of The Railway 9
Early Days at Blair Athole 15
The Engine Shed 31
Blair Atholl's Trains 39
Up and Down 49
Men and Machine 55
Blair Atholl Pictorial 69

Facets and Features

The Struan Bankers 75
Blair Atholl's Water Supply 81
Queen Victoria's Visit - 1863 89
Covering The Carriages 93
Summer Camps at Black Island 95
The Visit Of Crown Prince Hirohito 101
The Loading Gauge 103
A Fateful Hogmanay 107
Acknowledgements 109
Reference Sources 110

Head-on shot of the main station building in 1963.
(Howard Geddes)

A NOTE ON SPELLING
BLAIR ATHOLE OR BLAIR ATHOLL

By the time the railway was planned and built, the spelling then in general use locally, by the Duke and hence by all and sundry, was Athole and thus **Blair Athole** became the station's name, which spelling was duly reflected in the station's nameboards, in the railway timetables and on all paperwork and correspondence. In later years, the local spelling evolved to Atholl - the village, the estate and the Duke's title; the formal Valuation Rolls compiled for tax purposes recognised the parish as Blair-Atholl for the 1894-95 valuation year rather than Blair-Athole previously. The Highland Railway formally resolved to change the station's name to **Blair Atholl** on 7 September 1893, and this change was no doubt physically reflected on the station itself soon after.

It was common practice in those times to hyphenate double names, both place names and people's forenames, so that the station's name was written (in timetables and even the station nameboard) as **Blair-Athole** or **Blair-Atholl**. This hyphenation is therefore more than mere convention, and it could be argued that the village of Blair Atholl was served by the station of Blair-Atholl.

Throughout this book, I have tried to use the appropriate form of spelling according to context, although my convention has been to omit the hyphen.

There was a third, earlier, variation: **Blair Athol**. This form survives locally today only in the name of the distillery in Pitlochry, but it was used in the 1845 railway proposal. This spelling was also used for one of the most famous racehorses of all time. Foaled in 1861 in Yorkshire and achieving enduring fame winning both the Derby and St Leger in 1864, he was apparently named after the village, although I am unaware of any connection with the Athole estates. A Gresley Pacific locomotive built in 1925 was named Blair Athol, but it was definitely named after the horse.

In the 1790 Statistical Account, the place, village, parish or general area, is consistently written as Blair-Atholl or Atholl, yet the incumbent duke is consistently the Duke Of Athol. In the 1845 Statistical Account (written in June 1838, so no hint of any impending railway) the duke is now referred to as the Duke Of Atholl. Nowhere is there a reference to Athole. The National Gazetteer, 1868, has Atholl yet The Gazetteer of Scotland, 1882, has Athole. Maps of the 17th century have Athol. It must be concluded therefore that Blair Athole was a temporary variant.

A NOTE ON THE HILL

The incline from Blair Atholl to Drumochter has no specific formal name covering its entire length. It was locally and colloquially known simply as The Hill, although Struan Bank is occasionally used in railway documents.

BEFORE THE RAILWAY

Blair Castle has been a strategic location for centuries, guarding the traverse over the Grampian mountains for trade and travellers between the south and the northern areas of Scotland, although most travellers preferred the much longer but easier and less hazardous way around far to the east nearer the coast, or else indeed by sea. The first known route is Comyn's Road, built by John Comyn, Earl of Atholl and Badenoch, who was either father John the Black Comyn or son John the Red Comyn, in the latter half of the 13th century. The Minigaig Pass later supplanted Comyn's Road, but both went directly over the Grampians from beside Blair Castle to broadly where Kingussie is today. The distances are reckoned to be 27 miles for Comyn's Road and just over 25 for the Minigaig. They rose to a height of about 2500 feet and were impassable in winter.

Suitable as drove roads, little wonder these routes were not considered viable for improvement when General Wade surveyed the area for his military roads in 1724. His alternative route over Drumochter was about 42 miles in length, considerably longer but far and away more able to cater for heavy wheeled vehicles, and, by and large, passable.

A century or so later, Wade's military roads were repaired and improved by the Commission for Highland Roads and Bridges, a body set up by Parliament to execute an extensive programme of maintenance and new construction throughout the Highlands. Still today one of the country's most recognised engineers on a par with Isambard Kingdom Brunel, Thomas Telford was the Commission's appointed Engineer. He in turn employed the highly capable John Mitchell, originally a stonemason by trade, as "Chief Inspector and Superintendent of Highland Roads and Bridges" to oversee that work through a group of district inspectors. John Mitchell (1779-1824) was described by Telford as "a man of inflexible integrity, a fearless temper and indefatigable frame".

John Mitchell's son Joseph Mitchell followed in his father's footsteps, gaining practical experience as a mason working on the Fort Augustus Locks of Telford's Caledonian Canal. He clearly was as capable as his father and, having caught the attention of Telford, he became his clerk and studied engineering. John Mitchell died in 1824 from the exigencies of his work, and Joseph Mitchell succeeded to his post of Chief Inspector at the age of only 21. In 1828 he was appointed engineer to the Scottish Board of Fisheries, where he was responsible for the construction of 16 harbours across Scotland under their harbour building and improvement scheme. He came to have a particular interest in railway construction and, from the late 1830s, was involved in surveying routes of new lines and promoting their execution.

If there is one man responsible for the building of Blair Atholl's railway, it is Joseph Mitchell. Indeed such were these men's reputations, that when the railway did come to Blair Atholl, George, 6th Duke of Atholl, who could hardly bear to think of his estates being sullied by anything so public as a railway, was mollified by the thought that since John Mitchell had built the road through the estate to the entire satisfaction of his grandfather John, 4th Duke, then, like father like son, Joseph Mitchell would achieve the same happy result.

And so, with high reputation and that background of successful projects and spurred on by a survey (by someone else) for railway routes throughout Ireland, Joseph Mitchell took it upon himself to do much the same for Scotland. It cannot be said that he succeeded, but in 1845, with the prospect of Aberdonians projecting a plan for a railway from Aberdeen to Inverness, Joseph Mitchell decided otherwise; he "being familiar with the country, and having taken levels for shortening the road by the Highland route to Perth, felt satisfied of the practicality of a railway across the Grampians in that direction" - in other words a railway from Inverness over Drumochter and through Blair Atholl. Furthermore, this would be for the benefit of Inverness by the people of Inverness. He noted it would be 65 miles shorter to the southern markets than the alternative via Aberdeen.[1]

A committee was formed in Inverness and on 24 March 1845 their prospectus was issued. The project was underway, shares were taken up, and the money rolled in - this was the time of the Railway Mania after all. It is worthy of note that whereas the Highland Railway is generally regarded as having its roots in Inverness and enabling the expansion of trade from the north to the south, this first Perth & Inverness proposal is subtitled "in direct continuation of the Caledonian, Scottish Central, and Scottish Midland lines" and the first named directors, Marquess of Breadalbane and Lord Belhaven, were respectively the Chairmen of the Scottish Central and Caledonian companies. Furthermore, the Duke of Athole is conspicuous by his absence. Indeed, as far as I can tell, no landowner south of Drumochter was involved (apart from the Marquess of Breadalbane in his capacity as chairman of the Scottish Central Railway). Even though many of those involved in the initial prospectus were based in and around Inverness, the whole thrust of the proposal was to reach Inverness from the south, for example:

This line will pass by the vicinity of the magnificent and picturesque scenery of Dunkeld, Taymouth, Blair-Athole, ... The crowds of visitors attracted annually to these localities ... will be greatly increased by the cheap and ready access afforded by this line.

A breathless pamphlet of some 28 pages extolling the virtues of the proposed Highland Railway (confirmation that that name was even then in current thinking for the undertaking) was published in 1846 by J. B. Fraser of Relig, Inverness-shire: "...the whole of Athole, from Dalnacardoch to Dunkeld, including the vallies of the Tummel and the Tay, presents a district the most luxuriant and fertile...". In contrast to the Prospectus, this pamphlet was much more geared towards the Inverness view; for instance some of the benefits of the railway were illustrated in the bringing of Athole's timber plantations to market, thus:

The plantations of the late Duke of Athole, which are understood to cover a space of 15,000 acres of soil generally favourable to wood; and a great proportion of which have attained or passed the age of 40 years, having during that period had the benefit of regular thinning and good management. The produce per acre, if gradually cut, including thinnings, cannot, under such circumstances, be held as over-estimated as average 400 trees, at 10 solid feet each, or 4000 solid feet. Now, as 50 solid feet, or thereabouts, of fir or larch, go to the ton, it follows that each acre should at this rate produce about 80 tons, yielding for the whole plantations the enormous total of 1,200,000 tons.

Again, as by sending these to market, an average of 24 miles by Railroad [i.e. to Perth], instead of in the usual way, there will be a saving of fourpence per ton per mile, it equally follows that the owner of these plantations would, in the course of their sale, pocket the immense sum of £480,000, in addition to the sale value, instead of sacrificing it in expenses of carriage by the ordinary way.

Thus, as affording an inducement to planting, the establishment of this Railway would entirely alter the aspect of the country; for where, as at present, the hopes of sale are now so small that few would incur the expense for so uncertain a benefit, on the Railroad being established, it

---

1 The part taken by Peter Anderson, solicitor, should not be forgotten. From a family prominent in promoting coach and railway communication in the Highlands over many years, it was he and Mitchell jointly who formed the promotional committee to issue the Prospectus for the Perth & Inverness Railway. He continued to be the solicitor for all the various railway promotions in the Highlands of Scotland, including the Inverness & Perth Junction Railway.

will ensure a certain market for every tree as it becomes ready for the axe.

The pamphlet also claims that the daily coach from Perth to Blair is generally well-filled and states that it is licensed to carry thirty-two passengers. Today, it is rather hard to imagine that number of people (and their baggage) on such a vehicle of those times. However, the I&PJR in their Traffic Estimates of 1860 confirmed that figure and reckoned a 75% occupancy, being 2592 return journeys over 54 days per annum, meaning an estimate of 24 passengers per trip would transfer to the new railway.

With such high hopes, the Bill for the Perth & Inverness Railway was placed before Parliament, its first and primary component being a railway "leading from the City of Perth, by Blair Athol and Strathspey, to Inverness". Blair Atholl was on the railway map! However, John, 5th Duke of Atholl, or rather those running the Atholl estate[2], refused to even let the detailed survey go ahead over the estate. Joseph Mitchell overcame their objections, quite how isn't recorded, as well as those of the Seafield Estate where Lady Seafield "hated railways" and her husband did not demur, and the Bill went forward. However, it failed. It failed because of the audacity of Mitchell's plans - they were ridiculed:

Ascending such a summit as 1580 feet [being Drumochter, now measured at 1484 feet] was very unprecedented. Mr Mitchell, the engineer, was the greatest mountain-climber he ever heard of; he beat Napoleon outright and quite eclipsed Hannibal. He read a book the other day, of several hundred pages, describing how Hannibal had crossed the Alps; but after this line will have passed, he had no doubt quartos would be written about Mr Mitchell.

The preamble of the Bill was not proved. No Perth & Inverness Railway: the Parliamentary committee "had come to this conclusion with reference to the proposed altitude and engineering character of the proposed [railway]".

It would be another 18 years before the railway came to Blair Atholl.

The railway at Blair Atholl itself has to be considered in conjunction with the railway up The Hill to Drumochter. The Hill, or Struan Bank as it was also known, fundamentally shaped not only Blair Atholl railway station but also the village itself. In hindsight, Parliament probably erred too much on the side of caution, but understandably so - a railway higher than anywhere else, a main line steeper for longer than anywhere else, through country renowned for wild weather, using technology which, whilst not in its infancy, was still in its youth. Joseph Mitchell was clearly not sufficiently persuasive, and I do wonder if he underestimated the difficulties in getting trains over The Hill. When the railway was built, the facilities at Blair Atholl for assisting trains were scant, and the locomotives built especially for the line were not really up to the job, even after nearly twenty years of locomotive development since 1845, as we shall see. Eventually, The Hill and Blair Atholl were bound together as though one, with round the clock employment of men and machines based in Blair Atholl needed to keep the traffic moving on all occasions and in all weathers. The village would be a different place even today if not for The Hill.

But I have digressed. The Invernessians' strategy, with Mitchell's confidence being the force behind, remained the route over Drumochter, but their tactics were to achieve this in stages.

---

2   John, the 5th duke, was never mentally capable of running the estate's affairs. His nephew George Murray, then 2nd Lord Glenlyon, managed the affairs of Blair Castle; he had married in 1839 Anne Home-Drummond, daughter of Henry Home-Drummond who was one of the Trustees of the 'late Duke of Athole' whom I take to be the 4th Duke. The 5th Duke died on 14 September 1846 unmarried, childless and of unsound mind; George Murray then became the 6th Duke. Joseph Mitchell could have been dealing with the Trustees of the 4th Duke, the legal guardians of the 5th Duke, or the agents of the Atholl Estate through George Murray.

The story of the genesis of the Highland Railway and the railways radiating from Inverness has been told elsewhere, but from Blair Atholl's point of view, their new railway was approaching simultaneously from both north and south. First, at the Inverness end, the Inverness & Nairn Railway opened in 1855, a full ten years after the rejection of the Perth & Inverness plan. Then during 1858 the Inverness & Aberdeen Junction Railway extended the line to Keith to join up with the line from Aberdeen. At the Perth end, essentially independently of the Inverness contingent, the Perth & Dunkeld Railway opened in 1856 as a branch line off the main line to Aberdeen from the south. These railways served their local populations well, but still Blair Atholl was still without a railway.

The gap was destined to be plugged by the Inverness & Perth Junction Railway, but some parties involved were in combative mood. The story needn't be repeated here of the circumstances of the Great North of Scotland Railway establishing some of their Directors onto the board of the Inverness & Aberdeen Junction Railway and then being bought out. But mention must be made of the Duke of Athole being as equally fractious. By this time, it was George Murray, as the 6th Duke, now fully in charge of the Atholl estates. In 1850, naturally enough due to the estate's presence in Dunkeld, he became a Director and Vice-Chairman of the Scottish Midland Junction Railway who had been promoting their branch to Dunkeld, but it seems he had resigned when passed over as Chairman. When their promotion failed, out of the ashes a group of mainly local landowners was formed who did successfully prosecute their plans, this time for an independent Perth & Dunkeld Railway. But the 6th Duke of Athole was not involved and indeed his insistence that the revenue from his toll bridge over the Tay at Dunkeld be maintained became such an issue that Dunkeld's station was sited on the other side of the river at Birnam.

In this view from Garryside towards the hotel and village, there are no discernible signs of the railway, so it is thought to have been taken before the railway works commenced in 1861. Compare it with photo on page 12 where some outbuildings of the hotel visible in this photograph have been demolished.
(Blair Castle Archives)

The Coming Of The Railway

A committee to promote the Inverness & Perth Junction Railway (I&PJR) was formed early in 1860. Sensitive to the views of the Duke of Athole but with the need to have the railway on his lands for over twenty-four miles, Promoters and Duke met 9 June 1860. The Duke baldly stated he objected to all railways in the Highlands; he had opposed the 1845 scheme; and he objected still more to the prospect of a mere branch that ended in Pitlochry. But he left the way clear for negotiation because he added that if he were to consent to a railway at all then it would be as then proposed. Accepting that this was most beneficial to the general public, he declared that he needed to be satisfied that the line would not be detrimental to himself or his tenants - and his approbation seemed to depend only upon the actual route of the line.

The way was clear to satisfy all sides in providing a railway through Blair Atholl. Joseph Mitchell met the Duke at Blair Castle in September 1860, described in sometimes unflattering detail in Mitchell's *Reminiscences of my Life in the Highlands*. But those same *Reminiscences* go on to describe a classic of persuasion:

In the course of conversation, I remarked that it was thirty-six years since I first breakfasted in that room, and I then recounted my first interview with his Grace's grandfather.

"Ah! how odd," the duke remarked, "your father built the Tilt bridge and made the new road below the castle, and now you are come to make the railway." And the duchess said, " The young lady who brought you to breakfast is now Lady Oakley."

It was arranged that next day at eleven we should proceed to examine the line. In the carriage I laid out my plans. The duke said I had better explain to the duchess, she understood plans better than he did. Fortunately I had ordered the line to be staked out for several miles, indicating the direction by little white flags, which very much pleased his Grace, and I gained his confidence by explaining that by the line passing through a certain bank two or three fine oak trees would have to come down. He said he would not submit to that, he was determined; but the duchess, with admirable tact, threw oil upon the waters, and explained that in a wooded country some sacrifices must be made, and that his Grace, she was sure, had no want of fine trees, and could very easily spare a few for so important a purpose. He was, however, much pleased at what he called my honesty in explaining this.

His Grace had made a handsome new approach through his park of some two miles in length to the north of the castle, and as we could not carry our gradient of 1 in 70 without crossing the north end of it and cutting a little corner off the park, he was very decided in his objections. It would destroy his beautiful approach, which had cost him so much. I assured him it would not be seen, as we would go over it or under it; and besides, the company, I was sure, would give him a handsome lodge, so that the railway would be an ornament rather than an eyesore at the north entrance of his demesne. I drew a rough sketch of the lodge which might be made, and with which the duchess was much pleased.

His Grace accepted the railway over the approach.

Given that the Duchess was pleased, the Duke had no choice but to be pleased also. Thus, West Lodge was born. In modern parlance, one gets the feeling that Mitchell was winging it. What the said new company thought of this commitment isn't recorded, but West Lodge was indeed eventually built by the Highland Railway.

Similarly successful negotiation took place regarding the crossing of the Garry at Calvine, the innovative bridge-over-a-bridge result we see today. After this meeting, the Duke's attitude to the railway took an about turn very much for the positive, as Mitchell notes:

> *In fact, from that time, for nearly two years during the progress of the works, I seemed to have secured his goodwill and confidence, and he insisted on my being his guest whenever my duties brought me to Athole.*
>
> *As to the valuation of his land, he would not allow a law agent to interfere. He would leave all to Mr. Elliot, a gentleman extensively employed by railway companies on land valuations, an honest and upright arbitrator.*
>
> *He took great interest in the works, which seemed to give him a new pleasure, and had he lived, from his desire to do right and the interest he began to take in public matters since the railway began, he would have proved a valuable man of business; but alas ! it was not to be. He was seized with cancer in the throat, from which he suffered great agony. He bore his fate with a manly and intrepid spirit.*
>
> *Although very ill, he insisted on travelling on the line. And on the eve of its being opened a truck was fitted up for him, and, accompanied by the duchess and myself, we travelled between the County March and Pitlochrie, and he seemed to enjoy the rapid motion in descending from the County March at the rate of fifty miles an hour—rather a dangerous speed on a new-made line.*

The Duke took shares in the I&PJR and became a Director. When the Bill for the building of the I&PJR was accepted to go before Parliament, thus making its successful passage through virtually certain, on Friday 8 March 1861 the Duke was enthused enough to dispatch a telegram to the Duchess rejoicing that "The preamble of the Highland Railway has been proven, have the Bells rung". The Duchess didn't respond in perhaps quite the way expected given her prior enthusiasm and persuasion, for on the following Sunday she eloquently wrote back:

> ...*we rung my little handbells, told the children & danced about the room - but we never seriously imagined that you intended they rung the tower of the Cathedral, to peal forth its joyful notes on the occasion of a <u>moreinary irruption</u> being permitted to change the face of all nature around - nor do I suppose you did. Anyway it would have been <u>impossible</u> as the Garden lads could never have turned out in the dark to sound anything but <u>discord</u> ....* [the Duchess' own underlining]

And possibly mindful of his wife's obvious awareness of local sensitivities, the Duke didn't capitulate entirely to his new-found affinity with the railway. The Minutes of the I&PJR record days before the opening of the line

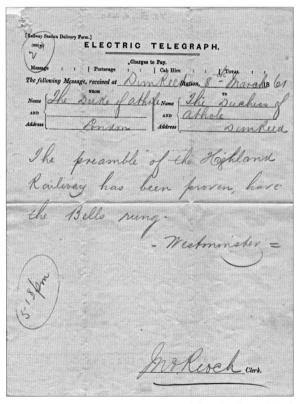

(Blair Castle Archives)

a strong representation from the Duke concerning compensation for himself and his tenants, and arguments of one sort or another rumbled on for years between the railway and the 6th Duke and his son and heir the 7th Duke, thus achieving an admirable balance between the railway's protagonists and antagonists; no mean feat.

The 6th Duke's death is recorded in the I&PJR's Minutes on 16 January 1864:-

Announcement of the death of His Grace the Duke of Athole, a Member of the Board, and they desire to record the high sense they entertain of the great and valuable Services rendered by His Grace to the Inverness & Perth Junction Railway Company - he having supported the undertaking from the commencement when it was surmounted with difficulties, and when his valuable assistance was almost vital to its success - and so long as he was able continued to render it most efficient services and to take a lively interest in its prosperity. The Board direct the Secretary to transmit an excerpt of this minute to the Dowager Duchess of Athole.

But meanwhile, works were progressing - fast. The Bill was passed on 22 July 1861 and work formally started on 17 October 1861 with the cutting of the first turf at Forres. Mitchell divided the work into nine contracts, that for Blair being awarded to Alex Wilson & Sons, Granton (Midlothian) at £58,771-13-2d. Blair Athole station itself didn't present any particular problems; the line ran right alongside the rear wall of the Blair Atholl Hotel, there being ample room for the facilities to extend width-wise on the flat towards the River Garry and plenty of space to the west until the railway crossed the Banvie Burn. However, the bridge over the Tilt was a significant structure. An I&PJR drawing exists of what has to be the bridge as originally intended; yet the stonework was actually built to a subtly different, and no doubt cheaper, design - more rectangular and without the curving stonework. There is a photograph of the

West Lodge as eventually built, a railway building just as much as an engine shed, even though having no railway purpose at all. It's not known how close it was to Mitchell's original sketch which persuaded the Duke to accept the railway through his grounds, but it's certainly a romantic design. There is an unattributed sketch in the Castle Archives but it's so similar to the structure above in terms of ground levels and the stepped side wall that it more likely to have been drawn after the building was built rather than be Mitchell's basis for the building. It was also agreed that a "suitable boathouse" be built at Woodend upon demand: another unlikely railway building, were it ever built. (Howard Geddes)

viaduct under construction but unfortunately it is a distant view and the close-up isn't suitable for publication.

As early as 18 July 1861, claims for compensation were being submitted. In Blair Athole itself there were four: William West, Robert McLaren saddler, Malcolm MacFarlane innkeeper and Andrew Low meal miller (extract from a List of Tenants of the Duke of Athole who agreed that the Arbiter shall determine their compensation), plus a fifth concerning the Glebe across which the railway ran. This is not to say they were settled quickly – as mentioned above, the Duke had to press for progress. By the end of 1861, the Duke had agreed to several of his quarries supplying material to the railway – one was Tulloch Quarry (Shierglas). As well as stone, the Duke also supplied the wooden sleepers, his payment being £3,000 in stock.

As can be seen from the map of 1865 in the next chapter, the facilities at the station were simple – nothing like they developed into in later years. There was a wooden shed that would shelter two locomotives of the time. The Timetable upon opening showed there was one train which left Blair Athole in the morning and returned at night, implying that the locomotive was stored at Blair Athole overnight thus justifying the shed; a couple of months later there were two trains leaving Blair Athole in the morning and returning at night so two engines would be needed and neither would be available to assist during the day. The shed would contain both of them overnight. This suggests it wasn't intended at the outset to have engines available, let alone dedicated, to assist trains up The Hill. Water for the engines was stored in a cast iron tank on a very substantial stone base, set adjacent to the main line beside the mill lade. The arrangements for the coaling of the engines is a complete mystery.

Railway works are in evidence, but clearly unfinished. The station building appears in a later photograph in the same position, so it must be one built to the standard template that the Board accepted for temporary station buildings to be provided upon the line's opening.

It's very difficult to make out on the original photograph, but the vehicles in front of the Atholl Arms seem to be the contractor's locomotive and six-wheel tender: a vertical object on its left looks like its chimney rather than a post or water column behind.   *(Blair Castle Archives)*

The railway tracks provided were little more than a loop of a considerable length, so that trains could pass. The goods yard laid out from the start essentially remained the same until it was lifted in the 1960s. With the need for two passenger trains to be held overnight, it's probable that the siding beside the main line was used for that purpose rather than for its use of holding goods vehicles in later years. There was a little stub, quite strange really but possibly for end-loading of road carriages and/or for loading horses, and a siding for the loco shed which included a small (very small) turntable. It's been stated that the turntable was 20 feet in diameter, although the Minutes of 7 February 1865 record there was a turntable of 16 feet diameter at Dalwhinnie "now lying unemployed" which conceivably could have been brought down to Blair Athole. Whichever size, the turntable was too small to turn the tender engines in use at the time, although even the 16 feet diameter one could at a squeeze turn an engine and its tender separately, which was common practice at the time however inconvenient this might appear. It is unclear whether one was installed at the opening.

At the beginning, a simple timber building on the Up side served as the main facility – installed in time for the opening, it was soon modified, because the open area which can be discerned in a pre-opening photograph has been enclosed. At some stage, perhaps from the opening, a new waiting shed had been provided on the Down side – this can be seen in early photographs; it remained for many years into the 1930s until replaced by the waiting shed there today.

I would say these were the original facilities. There was no goods shed and the goods yard was bare of the buildings that came to be there in later years. The very long siding, I suggest, is an afterthought; its length being the same as the loop clearly shows that it was intended to hold a northbound train whilst another train overtook. This implies that quite soon after opening The Hill was a bottleneck, with trains having to be held at Blair Athole whilst the single line cleared.

Thus, when it first opened for business, Blair Athole station was a straightforward affair with no especial facilities for the assistance of trains up The Hill but right from the start recognised as the terminus for local trains from Perth. There was no accommodation for the staff and hardly any facilities to keep any vulnerable goods from the weather whether they were inbound awaiting delivery or outbound to be loaded for shipment.

The railway had arrived and was open for business, but facilities were spartan.

New station from Tulach Hill, with rolling stock already in evidence. The temporary wooden engine shed can be seen in front of the hotel; the temporary timber station building and rather more permanent waiting shed on the other platform are both installed. There is no goods shed yet but there is the little shed that lasted until around 2010. Note Blair Castle, the footbridge over the Garry and the dwelling in the foreground. (Blair Castle Archives)

Early Days at Blair Athole

Blair Athole station was opened for traffic on Wednesday, 9 September 1863, when the Inverness & Perth Junction Railway (I&PJR) finally completed the connection between Inverness with the South over the Grampians. As with many projects even today, that didn't mean everything was ready; on the contrary hardly anything other the basics was ready. The I&PJR missed their hoped-for opening in time for the 1863 summer season; even the opening planned for the previous week was delayed because the Government Inspector was unexpectedly unable to execute his formal inspection planned for Wednesday, 26 August. Nevertheless the building of 104 miles of railway over little more than two winters and one summer was no mean feat. The stretch from Dunkeld to Pitlochry had opened on 1 June 1863, and from Forres to Aviemore on 3 August 1863. It was always planned that the Inverness & Aberdeen Junction Railway (I&AJR) would operate the trains over the I&PJR, and their responsibility duly commenced on 1 June 1863, not just for the I&PJR line between Dunkeld and Pitlochry but also for the services over the Perth & Dunkeld Railway (P&DR) which were previously being operated by the Scottish North Eastern Railway (SNER), it having already been arranged that the I&PJR and the P&DR amalgamate (which formally occurred on 28 February 1864). Unfortunately, not only was there a physical gap but none of the locomotives for the new lines had been delivered in time. So, the I&AJR had to hire in engines, and this they did, from the Scottish Central and Caledonian railways (but not, it would seem, from the SNER; the Caledonian provided three at no charge). It's not clear whether similar arrangements applied to passenger and goods rolling stock.

By the time Blair Athole was opened, four or perhaps five new goods engines and maybe just the one passenger engine had been delivered to the I&AJR. All these engines were named, and their naming rather gives the game away, for they were local to where they worked. Thus of this initial batch, only No. 20 *Birnam* and No. 21 *Forres*, both 2-4-0 goods engines, would have been available, with (doubtfully) a third 2-4-0 No. 22 *Aviemore* arriving at the very last moment. This suggests that the hired engines continued to be employed by the I&AJR. As likely as not, one would be employed on the Blair Athole - Perth service meaning it would be shedded overnight at Blair Athole, and of course others would work through Blair Athole. The same might apply to the passenger coaches on that service too.

More engines, both 2-4-0 goods and 2-2-2 passenger, were delivered and entered service during October 1863 and clearly the engine shortage eased. But operations did not get off to a happy start.

On the first day, the first service train from Perth, which was hauled by SCR 2-2-2 No. 9 got to Struan and stuck "in a mountainous country, unknown, in the dark, within hearing distance of the adjoining Falls of the Garry". The Duke's Factor John Robertson reported to His Grace

My Lord Duke   from: Athole Arms Hotel   at: 10.00pm

The train from the north has just come. The Stoppage has arisen entirely from the first Goods train going north having been too heavy and stuck on the hill about Dalnacardoch. This delayed all the south going trains as the telegraph was not working rightly at Kingussie and Dalwhinnie, and they could not safely move from any station until the trains from the south had arrived at that station. Another train is coming from the north, and after its arrival the trains detained at Struan and here can move northward. It is thought that Gilbert will have the telegraph all right

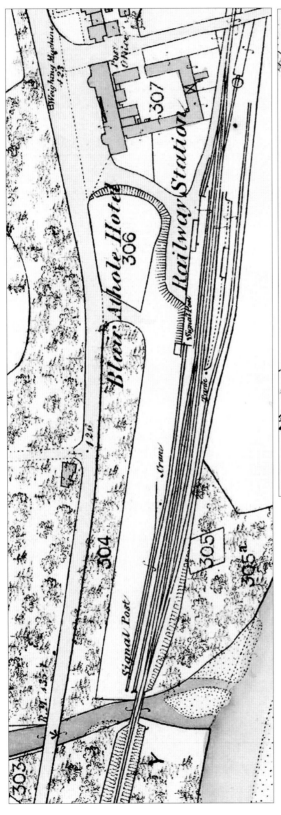
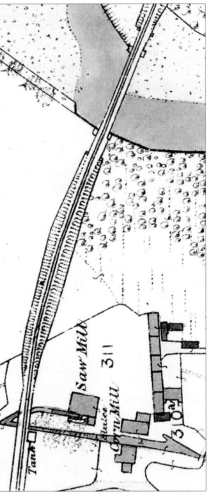

Blair Athole Station about 1865

OS 25" map "surveyed 1860 published 1867" and already printed showing the line to belong to the Highland Railway; thus this is a post-1865 layout. However, it is unlikely to differ from 1863.

The main station building is yet to be built – the map shows the temporary wooden shed. But the waiting shed on the northbound platform is present. There are no workmen's cottages in the station yard.

(courtesy National Library of Scotland)

tomorrow and that they will be able to start all right from each end to-morrow morg. The 4.10 train from Perth arrived at Blair here about 9 and I suppose it mite start as the local train from this [station] to-morrow morning. The passengers are quite furious.

I remain Your Grace's very respectful servt   John Robertson

The 2-2-2 wheel formation of the passenger 'Glenbarry' class with large 6' 1½" drivers and 14 tons of adhesion was most unsuitable for climbing gradients – the engines were intended for fast and light passenger trains. Contrast the 2-4-0 'Small Goods' class with 5' 1½" drivers and 22 tons of adhesion - intended for slow and heavy goods, and much more suitable for plodding up inclines. From the letter above, it looks as though even they were easily enough overwhelmed. Little engines were being put to big tasks that must often have been beyond them. This was recognised, because starting in 1872 these 2-2-2 engines were altered to 2-4-0. But the couple of conversions on the southern main line reigned for only two years before being supplanted in time for the 1874 summer season by 4-4-0 'Bruce' series of the 'Duke' class engines which were a magnitude more advanced and up to the job. 2-2-2 No. 33, introduced in October 1863, was named *Atholl*, and another 2-2-2 No. 51, built May 1864, was renamed from *Cluny* to *Blair Atholl* in 1874 shortly before being rebuilt to a 2-4-0. This was the only engine named after the village of Blair Atholl - and it was spelt thus even though the station was then named Blair Athole.

Nonetheless, on 24 September 1863 the I&AJR reported that the trains were now working with regularity, and it then submitted a list of claims amounting to some £40 from quite furious passengers "who had been detained through the irregularities" during the first 2 days. The claims were paid in full.

The I&PJR clearly had been determined to get their line open as soon as possible, for their Minutes for 14 August 1863 recorded that a "proposed demonstration on the opening of the line be postponed". Joseph Mitchell noted that a trip from Perth to Kingussie (and back?) had taken place on 6 September 1863, hauled by Scottish Central Railway 2-2-2 No. 12 and consisting of three first-class coaches and a brake van, he also noted that "the directors commenced the traffic

*2-4-0 No. 20 ex-*Birnam *of the Small Goods class, one of the original engines that would have worked the new main line in 1863, significantly altered by David Jones in 1872. Behind is No. 11 an earlier engine of the Seafield class built in 1859.*   (HRS collection)

The new station building has at last replaced the temporary wooden hut; and the first station cottages have now been built. Sidings are populated with wagons, and the water columns can be made out at the end of each platform. Can be dated to being before 1878 because the cottage by the level crossing hasn't yet been built.
(Author's collection/enlargement GWW F0180XA)

- an adventurous proceeding, for no preliminary trains had been run through to test the line and the working of the engines; and the men were new men unacquainted with the line and the gradients". Furthermore he noted that Dunphail had had no trains and no communication at all that first day. Nevertheless, we have seen how, the day before, the dying Duke and the Duchess apparently acted as test pilots – it turned out, despite Mitchell's misgivings, to be safe at 50mph since neither did they fall off their truck nor did the truck fall off the line. One wonders at what speed they came through Blair Athole! In retrospect this trip was decidedly risky, because the I&AJR recorded two accidents in the next month, one of which hinted at the need for fettling the fresh-laid line:

> On 5 October 1863, two empty wagons on the 4.20pm Up Goods Inverness to Perth derailed between Dalnaspidal and Struan. The cause was that the line was too narrow a gauge, being measured at 4'8" instead of 4'8½". Normally, track gets spread not narrowed, so this must have been a cause for concern.

> On 7 October 1863, a coal wagon suffered a broken axle on the 4.20pm Up Goods Inverness to Perth (again), this time between Struan and Blair Athole. The result was 14 wagons off the line which was "much damaged", although there was "no delay to passenger trains". This at least had nothing to do with the state of the track.

Mitchell is critical of The Hon. Thomas C. Bruce, chairman of the I&PJR, for pushing the line forward too much. He waspishly noted that Bruce "ably devoted about ten days per annum of his time to the service of the company", and goes on to say that the opening of the line, on the same day that the Government Inspector passed the line as fit to open, was much against his will and gave rise to much anxiety. After describing the large body of men keeping a close eye on the new permanent way and the unfinished watercourses on The Hill and relieved that the winter was not a severe one with no accidents or incidents arising, he offers a warning to others "not to interfere as Mr Bruce did, obstinately, in matters so purely professional as the opening of a new line". He strongly implies that Bruce was primarily responsible for what appears to have been a stroke Mitchell suffered in 1862, causing him to reassess his business arrangements. The enormous effort of building one of Britain's most spectacular lines in such a short time nearly took a fatal toll on the man who probably had the greatest influence in opening up northern Scotland's communications of all sorts.

I will describe the local train services to Perth in a later chapter, but it didn't take long for requests for intermediate stations to be received. On 2 December 1863 the Board considered a "Memorial from the Inhabitants of the district between Pitlochry and Blair Athole praying that

2-2-2 No. 32 Cluny of the Glenbarry passenger class before rebuilding but not quite in original condition, representative of the first engines designed for the Perth to Inverness main line. (HRS collection)

This view was taken on the same occasion as the previous photo and therefore is before 1878. This is a small portion of the original plate, concentrating on the wagons in the goods yard, and showing the newly built long stone wall with the Duke's newly planted lime trees. The blemishes are on the original glass plate.
(Author's collection/GWW E1779)

This shot can be dated to being after 1878 because the cottage by the level crossing is now built. Plenty of wagons are around; the goods yard is developing, now with a yard crane and possibly the next batch of station cottages in the process of being erected.
(Author's collection/GWW E0925XA)

a Station may be erected at Aldgirnaig adjoining the West Entrance of the Pass of Killiecrankie". This was successful; called Killiecrankie, the station was opened 1 July 1865. On the other hand, on 25 January 1864, there was another "Memorial praying for a Station at the Bridge of Garry for the accommodation of the Strath Tummel District". This was turned down.

Traffic patterns settled down over that first winter, the Directors declaring in their first two half-yearly reports after the line had fully opened that "Your Directors are happy to be able to state that the traffic in every way exceeds their expectations, and the prospects are most encouraging" (27 October 1863) and "… there is a Local Traffic as yet quite undeveloped…" (30 March 1864). Blair Athole station was set fair for a prosperous future.

The Saga of the Station Building and Engine Shed

Meantime however, most ancillary building works were outstanding, so much so that the stations were unfenced with completely unrestricted access, and indeed photos show that situation at Blair Athole. On 3 October 1863, the Engineer was instructed "to close up the front of all the Stations on the Line with Timber boards". This might have meant enclosing the open waiting area which is visible in the very earliest photos of the wooden Station Building, but it could also be interpreted as requiring the erection of the familiar picket-style station fencing enclosing the station as a whole.

Early on during construction, a "model plan for temporary stations along the line" was costed at about £80 per building. The simple timber hut visible at Blair Athole in early photographs, in its correct position prior to the line's opening and still there after opening, is evidence that this is one of those temporary station buildings. The photos also show that after the line opened it has been subject to alteration, compared to its state during construction. This temporary hut lasted for some years, as we shall see. It is possible that the alteration alluded to above was that considered on 16 March 1867 to alter the waiting shed on the "West Platform" [sic] at Blair Athole to "conform to sketch now submitted". Pity the sketch hasn't survived! I surmise that the portion open to the fresh air, albeit roofed over, is a waiting area for passengers, having what looks like bench seating along the rear wall. I can well imagine the complaints, especially over the winter.

It's not entirely obvious, but I infer that none of the railway staff, in particular the Station Master, lived in these station buildings. Rather, it was intended that they live in separate cottages. On 24 September 1863 plans of cottages for Station Masters and Porters at different Stations was "ordered to lie on the table" whilst the Company asked the Great North of Scotland Railway for the plan of the equivalent cottage at Rothiemay Station and how much it cost. Quite why Rothiemay Station was so attractive to the I&PJR I cannot say. Meanwhile the Engineer was "empowered to purchase from the contractors as many Huts as may be necessary for the temporary accommodation of the Company's servants". Bear in mind that this was nearly three weeks after the opening of the line. Soon, on 3 October 1863, "Mr Paterson submitted Plans for Cottages for Station Masters and Porters, which as revised by the Meeting were approved of and passed, and the Engineer was instructed to proceed with the buildings as soon as the weather will permit in the Spring". In the meantime, staff at Blair Athole were presumably put up locally.

Accordingly, on 6 February 1864, advertisements were arranged for tenders for the Station Masters' Houses and Porters' Cottages, and these were reviewed by the Engineer and considered by the Board on 30 March 1864, when that from Mr. Robertson of Dunkeld was accepted: "for the Cottages to be erected between Dalguise and Newtonmore inclusive

– the Station Masters' Cottages being £326 each, and the Porters' Houses £190 each". This would have included Blair Athole, of course. The Porters' houses are probably the terrace of four in the goods yard (note that the early OS does not show them); the site of the Station Master's house is less obvious, and I conjecture that Blair Athole's was never built, provision of accommodation being deferred until the main station building with domestic accommodation included was built.

The Duke's Factor soon began complaining about the state of works at Blair Athole. Perhaps some leeway had been allowed over the winter. The first letter I have seen is dated 8 June 1864 bringing attention to the fact that "the temporary Engine Shed at Blair Athole was sanctioned by the Duke on condition that a stone building of a proper design should be erected to the west … not be seen from the Castle". This shows that the wooden engine shed was always intended to be temporary and implies that it was always planned to be replaced by a permanent one, but begs the question as to the circumstances under which the shed needed sanctioning in the first place. Was it part of the original scheme, or was the storage and servicing of engines found to be necessary at some later stage, maybe even as a result of the company's experiences up The Hill after opening? Also, a stone wall was to have been built along the boundary of the line, all the way from near the Tilt to the Banvie Burn on the northbound side, the entire length and more of the station, at least half a mile – photos show that the railway delayed building it for as long as they get away with but it was eventually built. But the factor complained specifically that "The Company was also to build a stone wall along the side of the line through the Sawmill Yard at Blair" – it seems this stone wall was never built.

In the same letter (8 June 1864) the Factor says: "The making of the tramway to the Castle, I need not allude to at present." This is the only known mention of such an enterprise. Its route would most likely have been through the secondary Estate entrance beside the goods yard and past the Home Farm, but to exactly where and for what purpose is unexplained and entirely conjectural.

The first intimation of trouble was when the Duke's Factor John Robertson grumped to the Duke's solicitors on 3 October 1864: "The works on other properties along the line have been scrupulously attended to while these on the Duke's land have been, apparently, deliberately neglected". Work on the lodge at Bruar [West Lodge] had not begun, so that the keeper had to live elsewhere, the west end cutting was unfinished and the road had yet to be diverted – in other words, the railway had cut through the road from the Castle down to the Blair – Bruar road at the site of West Lodge, and nothing had been done to build the promised bridge over the railway.

Ten days later: "The ground on which they propose to build the Engine Shed … is not in their possession". This ground appears to be on the far side of the Banvie Burn, not today's site at all. The factor accuses the Railway of exaggerating the difficulties of the west side, and notes that they intend to apply for more land for sidings on the south side of the station, but "we must bind them to no buildings on that".

Nothing comes of these grumbles. On 8 April 1865 Robertson notes that "it is clear that they [the railway works] cannot be finished by the time the [7th] Duke comes to live at Blair".

Indeed, on 29 December 1865, Andrew Dougall the General Manager of what is by now the Highland Railway, replied to the Duke's solicitors thus:

1. As to the works of the west approach to Blair Castle, the Engineers say that these are finished, and therefore I will be glad to know what Mr. Robertson thinks should further be done by the Company – you are aware that the Company have erected a very handsome lodge at a considerable cost at this west approach which is not mentioned in the Agreement at all, and the Directors think this fact should not be overlooked.

2. *The Station Buildings at Blair* – The Company have no objection to adopt the modified plans sent by Mr. Robertson, but in consequence of the state of their Finances the Directors propose to postpone for a little the actual commencement of operations.

3. *Temporary Engine Shed at Blair Athole Station* – To place this Shed at the place for erection west of the Banvie Bridge would involve considerable expense, which the Directors do not feel warranted in going into at present, and they will rather consider the propriety of running the local trains from Pitlochry instead of Blair Athole, thus rendering a Shed at the latter station almost unnecessary.

This is a robust reply, containing the significant threat of withdrawal of local trains from Blair Athole. John Robertson peevishly states to the solicitors that the Pitlochry threat is "too weak to notice". He had a point.

The Duke wrote to the Highland Railway on 18 January 1866, gently prodding them about the Station Building but going full blast on the Loco Shed. First, the Station Building:

The Claimant [the 7th Duke] ... gave his approval of modified and much less expensive plans of Station Building at Blair than those which were approved of by the late Duke".

The reply a few days later was yet further delay:-

Plans of the proposed permanent Station Building at Blair Atholl were lately submitted to and approved by the Noble Claimants. The Company have not yet been able to give effect to them but they will of course do so as soon as they are in a position to proceed.

No plans for Blair Atholl's station building have come to light, so it isn't possible to say whether the current building is a simplified version of a more grandiose design. But as built, it is as good as identical to some station buildings on the Inverness & Ross-shire extension from Invergordon to Bonar Bridge: Kildary, Fearn, Bonar Bridge and Meikle Ferry; also Tain, which

Tilt Viaduct when new, the fresh light unweathered stone and ironwork already dirtied by the smoke from engines passing over. In the 1950s a small chunk was taken out of the near arch by an out-of-gauge load of corrugated iron – the mark was still there years later and might still be there today.

(HRS Roberts collection)

A brutal enlargement of the original, but it manages to show the hotel complex, the new workmen's cottage, most of the village including Garryside, the corn mill and the saw mill, as well as the gasworks. The date will be in the 1870s – the gasworks was built in 1871 and the cottage had been built by 1878. The saw mill yard is looking tidier than normal. The long stone wall on the railway boundary looks quite new, and the Duke's recently planted lime trees are mere lollipop-shaped saplings.   (Author's collection/part of GWW E1050XA)

is simply a single-storey version of the others. These stations opened on 1 June 1864 and from an early photo of Tain with the contractor's engine still hanging around, it would seem that Tain's station building was built for the opening. This implies the others were too, so it must be concluded that the design for Blair Atholl's station building was simply copied as being imposing enough for the Duke's station. Other stations built immediately later, like those in 1868 on the Sutherland Railway to Golspie, were to a simpler more vernacular design, so could have been regarded as unsuitable for Blair Atholl; but anyway their designs were probably too late to be used.

Then the Engine Shed:

In 1863 an unsightly Engine Shed of a temporary nature was, with the permission of the late Duke, put up immediately behind Blair Inn [now Atholl Arms Hotel], and in close proximity to the village, and also in sight of the approach to Blair Castle. This permission was given by the late Duke on the express condition that a permanent building was immediately to be erected to the west of Banvie Bridge, and out of sight of the approach to the Castle. ... The old shed, however, still remains, and forms a most unsightly object, and is besides the cause of a great nuisance to the villagers in consequence of the smoke etc from the pilot engine kept always in waiting, and which prevents the villagers from getting their clothes properly bleached, and is otherwise the cause of much annoyance.

It's not possible to say whether the shed was put up before or after the railway opened for business on 9 September 1863, but we can see that by 1865 trains were regularly needing assistance up The Hill - indeed an I&PJR Minute of 7 February 1865 praises "the economical working" of the Blair Pilot Engine. The reply was unsympathetic and again threatened a move to Pitlochry:

The Company have no desire to maintain the shed in its present position longer than is necessary but its removal to the position pointed out in the Note would involve an amount of expenditure which the Company do not at the present moment feel themselves justified in incurring. They have however intimated that if the removal of the shed is insisted upon they will rather than remove it to the proposed site consider the propriety of for the future running their local trains from Pitlochry instead of Blair Athole as they have at the former station the necessary accommodation for their engines. This would no doubt entail an inconvenience on the district but it may be forced upon the Company if they are obliged to remove the Shed complained of.

Furthermore, the Company rejected "amenity compensation" and stated that "nuisance to villagers" is not good enough grounds for compensation [to the Duke]; with the shed only visible from a public road, the Duke himself has no view of it.

Notes internal to the Atholl Estate complained about the "continual passing and re-passing of the Engine" (note the singular – one engine). The Duke was advised that the engine shed and station building would be

Looking south towards golf club bridge in 1963, with the signs of damage still obvious. The other arch is damaged in much the same way too.
(Howard Geddes)

Another view from Tulach Hill. This is an enlargement of part of a GWW plate. There is a short double-headed train, with a variety of wagons, including a meat van, a tanker and a tarpaulined wagon where one can nearly make out the lettering and number. The meat van has an odd construction on its roof which overlaps the ends, and there is a van with step-boards, same as in the siding, which suggests they are brake vans of some sort – both have glazed doors at one end, the nearer of which is open. There are also four coaches three of which are shrouded in Carriage Sheets - see the eponymous chapter. These will be spare coaches kept at Blair Atholl to be used when the traffic demands. Two seem to be parked on the main line beside the engines, but given that one coach is completely sheeted they must be in a siding and this is almost certainly what used to be the loco shed road. Note the bleachfield in front of the cottage.
(Author's collection/GWW468X, which is an enlargement print from GWW B0468X)

Still just the one cottage by the level crossing, now the goods yard has the goods shed and various other huts – one looks like the coal merchant's office. The platforms are now spanned by a footbridge, the same as is there today. The Duke of Atholl's lime trees are growing well - compare them in other photographs. The Foreman's house has now been built - it is noticeably bigger than the adjoining cottages and as big as it is, it is clearly only one dwelling with just the one front door. Various passenger coaches can be made out in the sidings.
(from a postcard, author's collection)

This is a much later photo. Note that there now two cottages by the level crossing and the cottages towards Garryside that the Duke's factor claimed would "spoil a pretty village" have also been erected – this dates the photo as 1901 or later. Of note are the white level crossing gates with substantial king posts, giving access to the sawmill. The Duke's limes are mature and still there, so a date of exactly 1901 won't be far out. *(Author's collection/GWW C5624)*

"attended to" within three years of 28 March 1866, but he demurred. This wasn't good enough; he wanted 1 August 1868, pointing out that five years from the opening of the line was long enough. He told his representatives to get on with it and get that agreement.

Maybe there were a few more private words for, on 9 May 1866, a fixed date was agreed to sort out the Station Building and Engine Shed, 1 August 1868 being eventually agreed as binding. But the agreement was that the existing wooden shed (temporary) should be moved (to remain temporary for ever, no doubt) to the west side of the Banvie Burn. Binding agreement or not, the railway not only failed to give a letter of guarantee, but also applied to the Duke for permission to build a new Engine Shed on the east side of the Banvie. The Factor noted on 11 January 1867 "quiet talk about removing the Engine Shed and Turntable to Pitlochry" and added in pencil that he hadn't even received a guarantee that the Station Building would be built as agreed. At last, on 28 February 1867 the Arbiter seems to have managed to extract a guarantee from the Railway, but the HR still pushed its luck by asking for a 1 January 1869 deadline. The Duke declined, and finally the HR acceded.

But the old Engine Shed remained - its transitory nature is obvious in several photographs where five timber baulks can be seen clearly propping up the south side wall, with presumably a similar set up on the other side which is out of sight (a similar situation occurred at Helmsdale, but in that instance the shed did fall down). Following yet another complaint, this time to the Arbiter, who, on 28 March 1867, found that the HR was not bound to remove the shed until the 1 August 1868 deadline for the new shed, but the HR did concede that if at all possible they would remove it before that date. The HR's reluctance was palpable. They must have had their fingers crossed when they agreed to 1 August 1868, because

> HR minutes 18 May 1867: 10 inst report: transmitting plans and estimate of a new Engine Shed, TT & necessary sidings at BA - Est of £2848-10-1d. Resolved to postpone doing anything in these works for 12 months.

After a letter from the Duke to the HR on 20 December 1867, where he must have complained yet again that nothing had happened, at last the Board on 1 January 1868 resolved:

> To erect Engine Shed forthwith but endeavour to have the time for erecting the new station extended to 31-12-1869. Mr Buttle (the HR's Resident Engineer) authorised to take down ½ Keith and use masons, thus reducing cost to £575.

We can reasonably conclude that the Loco Shed was built during the summer of 1868. Presumably the old Shed was simply destroyed. It is not clear what happened to the old Turntable (presumably scrapped as being of no use), but it seems that two new 'large' turntables had been acquired back in 1866 from Messrs Cowans, Sheldon & Co, Carlisle at £280, one for Blair Athole and one for Grantown. Blair Atholl's turntable must have lain around in its wrapping paper for quite a while. The siding remained for a long time after, at least until 1884.

It has been stated that half the engine shed at Keith was moved to Blair Athole. I believe this gives slightly the wrong impression of a careful stone-by-stone transfer from one location to another. Instead, I feel it far more likely that part of Keith Shed was relatively carefully demolished, such that much of the resulting material could be reused in the building of Blair Athole shed. Such items as the big wooden doors and the half-round paned windows would almost certainly be recovered and reused - in fact it's one of those quirks that the height of the windows in many of the Highland Railway's engine sheds varied from shed to shed for no discernible reason, yet those at Keith and Blair Athole are the same, which rather supports my conjecture. Keith shed was originally a four road shed, and was 'nine-windows' long. Blair Athole is 'seven-windows' long with three more windows on the office side - making a total of ten windows. One can only wonder that the length of Blair Athole shed was determined simply by the numbers of windows recovered from Keith! Keith's shed was found to be in excess of requirements, and one can only speculate what might have happened at Blair Athole if an entire half a stone shed hadn't been deemed spare.

We can assume that the rebuilt Engine Shed, the Turntable and ancillary works were completed during the summer of 1868, to meet the deadline. But the same cannot be said for certain about the Station Building – the best that can be said is that it was built before the end of 1869.

Redevelopment of the Site: Workmen's Cottages

The removal of the Engine Shed left an empty site with a useless siding. This would never do! There is photographic evidence that the siding was pressed into use as standing for the coaches for the local passenger train. With the engine shed out of the way, the two long lay-by sidings were extended as far as they could go – right up to Ford Road, where three sidings, two long and one short, ended in a neat row of protective buffer stops.

But after a few years, the first building comprising two Workmen's Cottages was put up. This happened after 1871 when the gas works was opened and before 1878 when the building appears on maps. This building and its gardens were on the site of the two extended lay-by sidings, which obviously were cut back accordingly. It is a simple single-storey two dwelling building, with attic dormers and roof lights, facing south, designed in the vernacular by the

Highland Railway. An original drawing (dated 1894) has two lean-to privies, but photographs and other sketch plans show none.

There was a garden squeezed between the now-truncated two-track lay-bys and the Cottages. It was 63' 6" long, and can be seen used for putting out the washing - the bleachfield. This is ironic given the previously mentioned rows, especially as the old shed siding was still there, presumably still used or at least usable. Obviously, railwaymen's washing is impervious to smuts! If it's of any significance, there was a specific gap of 14ft left between buffer stops and the garden-end.

The whole was bounded on the south by a low stone wall, which is likely to have been built at the same time as the Cottages. It used to extend much further - right to the other end of the platform, and was truncated only when a third lay-by siding was put in, in late 1902. The Duke had planted Lime trees all along this wall "in the time of Mr MacGregor, forester", and a pretty sight they looked. It was with regret that they had to come down after the double-tracking to Drumochter in 1900 due to the subsequent extension of facilities. Compensation was paid to the Duke: loss of wood £40 and loss of screen from castle £60. That truncated wall is still there today.

After some years, in 1894, a second building for a pair of Workmen's Cottages was built alongside the first, in the latter's back garden. It was slightly bigger all round. There is a hint that the two lay-by sidings were further shortened slightly to provide sufficient space. Outside privies were provided, and it is likely that the older house's occupants were provided with the aforementioned lean-tos to replace the shed-at-bottom-of-garden dunny.

These two buildings, with four dwellings, have stood the test of time, and are lived-in today.

The northbound platform was extended over time to accommodate increasing train lengths – realistically it could only extend towards Ford Road. At some stage before 1878, the short siding that served the old engine shed was lifted, thus leaving space for the platform to be extended past the Cottages and right down to the level crossing.

The third long lay-by siding came later, as noted elsewhere. Some trackwork remains today deep in the undergrowth, with what are becoming substantial trees growing between the sleepers.

The first, smaller workmen's cottage of the 1870s, taken in 1963 showing an original dormer on the left.
(Howard Geddes)

The Engine Shed

The essence of Blair Atholl as a railway station revolves around the need for northbound trains to be assisted up The Hill (or Struan Bank as it was perhaps more formally named). Facilities for sheltering the assisting engines, for replenishing them with coal and water, and even for running repairs and maintenance, all had to be provided, as had equivalent facilities for the drivers, firemen and fitters. This all sounds obvious, but I believe it wasn't so obvious in 1863 when the line was first opened. There was a certain naivety that everything would be all right on the day, but as we have seen operations did not go ahead quite as smoothly as intended. There is little doubt that the opening of the line was achieved under some stress. The Glorious Twelfth deadline had been missed and winter wasn't far away, so perhaps the opening went ahead 'come what may' in order to avoid losing some six months of revenue until the spring of 1864. Nevertheless, the need for assistance up The Hill was probably regarded as necessary from the start, as was the need for a shed to house and protect a couple of engines.

The rudimentary shed, so annoying to the locals as well as the Duke, managed to serve its purpose for some five years until the far more substantial shed was built, along with its more comprehensive facilities. Even so, a lot of water has passed along the Banvie Burn, and the facilities for engines at Blair Atholl were very different in 1868 compared with those in the 1930s, say. This chapter looks at these earlier days, showing how the engine shed and its surroundings developed.

The photograph below shows the shed in its "as built" condition. The rear end wall is solid but otherwise the same as the entrance wall, with an open roundel and what looks like a chimney, presumably a stone smoke-pot. Those at the entrance can be seen in other photographs which show the style of rounded-top wooden doors typical of the Highland. Although there are no early photos showing the front of the shed, it is reasonable to assume that the doors-end of the shed didn't change. The main roof is of slate, with an almost full length louvered sub-roof, made out of what looks like battened transverse wood planks, certainly not slates. The sub-roof is quite squat.

There are some offices to the side, their roof simply being a downward continuation of the main roof. I cannot spot any chimneys, but there is at least one side window. Access was from inside the shed with possibly an external door adjacent to the main shed doors. The plan was probably similar to others around the system. No different from today, there are probably seven "standard" windows on the rail side of the main shed, and three on the river side.

The smoke that can be seen

The new shed in its "as built" condition. It was built in 1869 from materials made available when the shed at Keith was halved in size.
(from GWW B0487 in Author's collection)

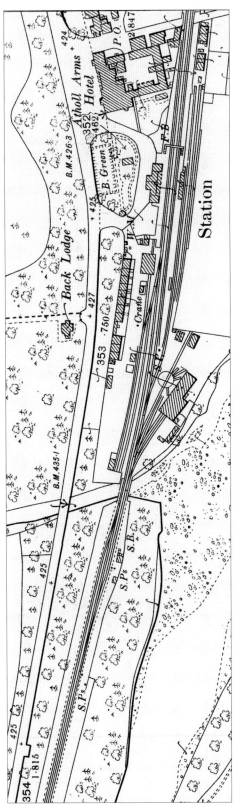
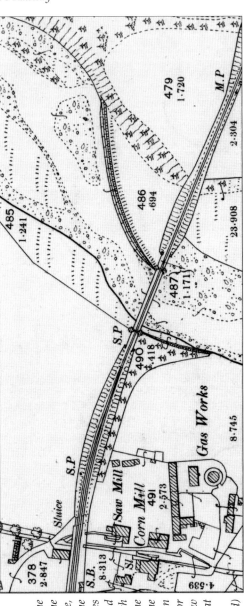

BLAIR ATHOLL STATION ABOUT 1900

There is still single track up The Hill, the second line being a lay-by siding. The facilities for the engines are still simple, with little more than the two-road engine shed and a single siding where engines can be replenished with coal and water and turned on the turntable. The wagons with the locomotive coal would be held in the short siding alongside. The four stubs off the turntable probably held the odd spare wagon or brake van, and possibly a snowplough or two. The two northbound sidings are now even more curtailed by the second cottage at their end.

(courtesy National Library of Scotland)

above the shed appears to be emanating from a locomotive on the main line: on the original photo, its chimney can just be made out above the shed window second in from the right.

Note how deep are the side and rear walls. The shed, including the side offices, has been built out from higher ground, the rail level being some eight to ten feet higher than ground-level beside the River Garry. There is a hint in the photograph that the walls below rail level are in fact retaining walls, there being a distinct "tidemark" along the nominal rail-level.

The ground has been long since been made up level with the railway, the River Garry/Banvie Burn confluence being pushed sideways somewhat to make room. I have been told that the infill is all cinders, built up over the years. In fact, I suspect the ground was deliberately raised in three stages, many years apart, as I shall show below. The water storage tank was still beyond the south end of the platform (broadly where the signal box is today), and it remained there for many years. I infer that a water column was provided conveniently outside the new engine shed, piped some distance from the water storage tank. The small turntable outside the original wooden loco shed also at the south end couldn't have lasted for long after 1868 when the shed was taken down, and from plans of the loco yard it would be reasonable to assume that the full-sized turntable (42') bought from Cowans, Sheldon in 1866 was installed at the same time as the loco shed itself in 1868.

The land form was still being recorded in an 1884 plan as being the same as the photograph. This and other plans show lands acquired in 1878, 1883 and 1884, the latter acquisition being over an acre behind the loco shed. This, initially, contained only an extension to the turntable road, some stores, and a new water tank (the original one still remaining at the east end). An 1892 plan shows this second water tank in place; interestingly, it also shows the original water tank still in place, but with a corner shaved off to clear the ever lengthening passing loop. If clearances were that close, perhaps the tank itself had been taken away (and reused on the loco yard water tank?) with only the mutilated base left behind.

There are surprisingly few known photos of the shed front without engines blocking the unencumbered full-on view of the original stone gable end and doors. The foreground loco is No.14397 **Ben-y-Gloe.** *Note the high shunt-signal; there was another one, just behind the camera, which was cut down to head-banging height for some reason.* (*H C Casserley collection*)

Engine Shed in later form in LMS days. The rear gable end still had doors, wide open as usual. Nobody ever seemed to close engine shed doors. They were when Bert Keller, in the 1950s, had to move a loco inside without much steam – he couldn't stop in time, so poked a buffer through the closed shed door. The smoke vents with their spindly umbrellas show there is space for four engines. Note the dormer structure: with one the other side, they supported the lifting gear that spanned the width of the shed; some quite substantial engine maintenance could be carried out. Two engines are sitting outside the front of the shed – the nearer is a Struan Banker, maybe No.15503; a third loco is being attended to at the back. There are piles of grey ash waiting to be taken away – a worker can just be seen 'tidying' the piles. The three wagons supply the coal – see how the siding is slightly raised. Coaling of the engines' tenders was done the hard way in the open with a shovel; later the siding was covered with a crude shelter, although exactly what level of increased comfort it provided is a bit of a mystery. (Author's collection)

The first build-up of ground around the loco shed must have been between 1884 and 1892, for the 1892 plan above gives an indication of more land in use. This would include the build-up around the rear of the loco shed, burying most of those deep retaining walls. This and another 1892 plan are interesting for they show proposals not only to extend the loco shed from two to four roads by building out sideways over the Banvie Burn but also to double the length of the existing shed – a tripling of its capacity if both were implemented, which neither were of course.

There is a late 19c. plan showing two structures beside the offices, one coach-sized, the other van-sized, making a cosy little quadrangle. There is an office extension and a wall or fence, probably delimiting or retaining the newly-raised area, which is broadly only at the front of the shed. One may surmise that whilst most of the 1892 expansion proposals were shelved (only coming to fruition in their final form with the 1898 line-widening), at least a small expansion took place, namely the addition of the "quadrangle". Hence the ground was built up then, the dormitory being indeed an old coach. There is even what looks like a privy (but possibly only an ash-pit) conveniently just around the back of the said wall.

On 6 July 1898, just after the doubling of the line up The Hill had been contracted (23 June 1898), the Ways & Works committee resolved to proceed with the purchase for £250 from the Duke of Atholl of an acre for a new turntable and a water tank - this must be the second water tank that was built in the loco yard, not the first (a second one had also been proposed in 1892, but never built). The land appears to have been taken in 1899, yet the land purchase was not completed until sometime in the summer of 1901, and not paid for until 1902. The final payment seems to have been for 9s/1d paid on 9 October 1902 by Postal Order!

On 7 December 1898, a £50 engine pit was authorised. Oddly, the 1892 Plan referred to above indicates that there were pits on the main line which were to be infilled and replaced with two pits elsewhere: whether this happened before the new pit was sanctioned or at the same time cannot be determined. The diagram reproduced on page 32 shows the loco yard layout at this time. Note what was probably the new engine pit just outside the shed, no doubt specially for banking engines on standby. This layout is either inaccurate or valid for a very short time, since the line is not shown doubled which happened in 1900. Note the quadrangle with the dormitory, here noted as a store and the continuing presence of the old turntable. The side offices have also been extended somewhat.

Various other packets of land were being obtained in various spots in 1899, 1900 and 1901, in support of the doubling itself, to accommodate extended sidings, the above loco facilities and more, as well as new workmen's houses. It is not at all clear what was built when, but things were certainly built in stages ("piecemeal" might be too strong a word.....). The intention was clearly to extend the existing turntable line between the loco shed and the main line to enable the second water tank and the new turntable (in a new pit) to be built, all without interfering with the existing arrangements, and to be done before the doubling of the line. For some reason, the turntable was not installed, apparently ending up at Daviot, presumably in connection with the gradual opening of the direct line between Aviemore and Inverness. Maybe no work was carried out until the land deal concluded in 1901, although it is just possible that some track was laid, but not the structures. Possibly, the land levels were being raised as land was

After the fire - although the main shed has been re-roofed, the engine shed offices are roofless and ruined with charred timber piled around. Just the other side of the Banvie Burn is the 'modern' pump house, itself looking the worse for wear from fire and rather obscuring that the shed's front gable end has now been demolished, leaving it open to all elements. There are now four lay-by sidings.

(J L Stevenson, courtesy Hamish Stevenson)

In BR days, around 1960, Perth-based Black 5 44924 is on shed; this is now just an open run-through. The burned-down offices have been replaced with a variety of utilitarian brick lean-tos. Locomotive coal stored in one or two open wagons is now protected from the wet by a rather crude corrugated iron shed. (HRS collection)

taken, all in preparation for the yard extension. With the 1901 acquisitions, the land owned by the Highland Railway reached its final extent.

The long stone wall, seen in other early photographs, along the railway's then boundary, was mostly demolished in 1903 to accommodate a new northbound siding. The Duke of Atholl had planted a long row of lime trees along this wall, all of which had to be felled and compensation given. Regret at this possibility was expressed in November 1902. Now, on 4 March 1902 a contract for slating the engine shed for £21-10-0d was agreed with two local chaps: Mr Falconer and Alex Cattenach. However, Alex and others were busy from summer 1901 to mid-1902 building a block of four workmen's houses (which still stand today) on Ford Road opposite today's preserved mill, and converting the six cottages seen in the photograph behind the goods shed into just three - bills were being submitted every month or two.

I have a summery photograph where the Ford Road block is built and occupied, yet, whilst there is an apparent boundary fence for the new land, there is no sign of the extended loco yard and the mature lime trees still stand guard over the station.

I suspect that the final expansion of the loco yard and lay-by sidings took place during late 1902/3. If this were to be the case, one of the first tasks would be to complete the raising of the level of the acquired land. An Ordnance Survey map of the time appears to confirm that this land reclamation to have been in progress in stages over the years. When the land had consolidated, the next task would be to substantially alter the loco shed, not only to knock out the rear wall entirely to allow two through roads, but also to improve the venting arrangements with a new sub-roof and four tall smoke-pots so familiar on Highland sheds. The new sub-roof was duly slated (by Falconer & Cattenach), shorter and higher than the previous version.

Further alterations are likely to have been the building of two dormer projections midway each side of the roof; these housed some form of lifting gantry inside the shed. Finally, the offices seem to have been extended from time to time, and I dare say something was tacked on about now. Falconer & Cattenach presumably did all the necessary re-slating.

The shed must have remained in this form for some time, with the familiar stone arches and doors at one end yet open to the elements at the other with a decidedly ugly wooden gable end. The yard was unusual, of course, in having two water tanks, cheek-by-jowl. Oil was kept in one, kindling in the other, and "facilities" grafted onto the outsides at some stage. The layout meant that there was plenty of unused ground, with an open expanse of neat cinder surface.

However, during the latter part of the last war the shed roof was entirely destroyed. This was the result of carelessness in that a can of burning waste, used to start up cold engines, was left near an oil drum. The oil drum exploded up through the roof, purportedly high into the air, whereupon it came back down again crashing through the roof. The upshot, apart from a startled village, was a burnt-out shed with no roof and ruined offices. The engine that was in the shed at the time was damaged, but not fatally.

The Canadian Army was highly active nearby lumber-jacking in the Atholl estate. They volunteered to replace the roof, but for some inexplicable reason were rebuffed, much to the annoyance of the enginemen (and the Canadians). Instead, the shed was left open to the skies for a while until a new roof was put on (by 1948). The ironwork came from Redpath & Brown in Motherwell, and whilst it looked new it appeared too narrow for the building, thus giving rise to rumours that it was second-hand. The roof cladding was definitely second-hand wood. The roof was formed as we see it today, with a double louvre. It was at this juncture that Tulloch Road was built from Ford Road, to provide road access to the site for the incoming building materials. I am told that this was when the ground level was finally raised. However, I am not convinced by this: I would suggest that the land was first shaped when the rearward extensions to the loco yard were built, in stages from 1884 to 1903, as I said above, with perhaps only minor earthworks being needed for the new road. Sadly, I have no photographs that can be reproduced showing the office side of the shed prior to the fire, indeed I only have one shot showing the old offices and even then they are roofless.

Said offices were left in a ruinous state until after March 1949, eventually being completely demolished and replaced with an ugly brick design; again that still is in place today. In fact houses were built all along Tulloch Road and still the offices gazed at the skies. In several post-war photographs, some old coaches-cum-vans can be seen right at the end of

1963, shortly after the track was lifted. Turntable pit in the foreground, eventual home to the rubble of the water tank bases. Crude coaling shelter behind and the loco shed in the background.
(Howard Geddes)

Snowploughs were stored in the yard for use when conditions demanded. An engine would be dedicated to the job of running up and down The Hill keeping it clear. One photograph has an HR 0-6-0 goods engine, known as a "Barney", so adorned.
(Author's collection)

the loco roads, presumably serving as temporary offices.

Sometime around the end of the war, a simple brick pump house was built by the Banvie Burn. Diesel-engined, the pump provided an alternative water supply to the shed and water tanks. Up till then, water had been piped down from the Fender Burn at Middlebridge (about a mile north) underground to the (site of) the old water tank at the south end of the station; thence it was piped to the other tanks.

After the engine shed and yard closed in 1962, the track was soon lifted and metal and the such recovered. The bulldozers moved in and swept the water tank bases into the turntable pit. However, they were prevented by the eventual owner from demolishing the shed itself, which still stands, even though the only original structures are the two stone walls above ground and any exterior stonework surviving underground.

"Can ye no hurry up yer sheep a bit — we've tae catch the 5.30 train at Blair Awful!"

Blair Atholl's Trains

The preponderance of traffic originating in or destined for Blair Atholl, whether that traffic be travellers or goods, is to and from the south. This has probably held true for all time. And much the same could be said for Pitlochry and Dunkeld. With the barrier of the mountains to the north, Blair Atholl was also a natural staging post in the journey over those mountains. In a railway context, this was ever far more than simply stopping for rest and replenishment; assistance was required to help trains get up and over The Hill - and this assistance took the form, of course, of extra engines attached to the trains.

This required, in today's parlance, extra infrastructure and resources. This was why there was a substantial engine shed and associated facilities, and also why there were lay-by sidings both northbound and southbound. Goods trains plodding north could be put to one side whilst fleet passenger trains kept to their important public schedules; and southbound goods trains having been barely kept in control down some twenty miles of steep hill could rest and recover – not least to let their brakes cool down!

With all these facilities to hand, it is completely natural that services primarily serving the Perthshire communities north of Perth would start and finish at Blair Atholl, rather than, say, Dunkeld or Pitlochry, now that there was a continuous line over Drumochter. But Struan/Calvine could have been considered as a railhead for the push up The Hill, and one wonders if that location was ever given serious thought. If it had and if it had won out over Blair Atholl as the place to receive assistance up The Hill, the impact on the two places would have been considerable. We shall never really know why Blair Atholl was chosen as the place, whether it was prosaically because the topology was more suitable or politically because of the proximity of Blair Castle and the Duke or simply that that was just the way it happened to happen, but the upshot was that Blair Atholl was the terminus for the Highland Railway's Perthshire services.

Local Passenger Trains

Right from the opening of the line, there was a local passenger service between Perth and Blair Atholl - initially one round trip a day, leaving at 8.00am and returning at 9.05pm. Three classes of passengers were carried: 1st class, 2nd class and 'Parliamentary'. Villagers were well served, with four other through trains heading south at fairly regular intervals, even a single train on Sundays; the northbound service mirrored the southbound. Apart from the local service, some of these through services could be used to achieve a day-return trip to Perth. There were separate goods trains too. A compressed timetable appeared in *The Times*, and presumably other national newspapers as well: it showed signs of haste in compilation with some mistakes and even a whole train service through Blair Athole omitted.

The timetable was very soon modified, with effect from 1 October 1863, with the local to Perth leaving at 7.50am. The summary timetable that appeared in *The Times* was still oddly compressed as well as inaccurate, with the return Perth to Blair Atholl local missing completely.

A third timetable came into effect from 1 December 1863, by which time the line had its expected complement of engines. Blair Athole now had two local services, leaving 7.50am and 11.30am and returning 6.15pm and 10.10pm. The 11.30am had been when the Mail from Inverness had come through: this through passenger service carrying the Mails seems to have been curtailed, with the Mail train arriving in Forres as usual but then carrying on to Keith (and

Aberdeen) rather than over Drumochter. This diversion was probably due to winter coming on, with the possibility of blocked lines and delayed Mail: this first winter was an anxious time with the line still unfinished and its ability to withstand fierce weather unproven. Blair Atholl's second local service both ways was mixed passenger and goods and this was reflected in the extra time allotted. They were slower because they might have to shunt goods wagons at every station, leaving passengers twiddling their thumbs meantime. There were now just two through trains each way, although it was still possible and practical to use one of them each way as one leg of a day-return to Perth.

Right from these early days, the passenger coaches (and the locomotives which hauled them) would be stored at Blair Atholl overnight, and as services developed in later years, at least one set of passenger coaches would overnight at Blair Atholl. In 1880 it is clear that two complete sets were still being based at Blair Atholl overnight, each doing one return trip, now with a third set based at Perth doing one return trip. In 1905, the Blair Atholl set comprised five carriages: 1 Brake-Third, 1 First, 2 Thirds, and 1 Brake-Van. An extra Third was added on Perth Sale Days: this set did two return trips a day. Another set did one return trip a day from Perth to Blair Atholl and back. Of course, these trains were primarily for passengers of the intermediate stations, because the people of Blair Atholl could also use the long-distance trains to and from Inverness. In fact the total service could be considered more than adequate - indeed quite excellent.

I have already stated that there was one spare carriage held at Blair Atholl for use upon Perth Sale Days. In fact, there were several spares because the Company distributed spare passenger carriages and even goods brake vans at strategic places throughout the system, to substitute in case of breakdown or to strengthen trains.

This means that there could be anything up to fifteen carriages scattered around the station, some in storage and some in active use. An interesting consequence of this was the need to protect these spare coaches – see the chapter on Carriage Sheets.

INVERNESS AND PERTH AND INVERNESS AND ABERDEEN JUNCTION RAILWAYS.

OPENING OF THE INVERNESS AND PERTH LINE THROUGHOUT.

Leave	A.M.	A.M.	P.M.	A.M.	Exp.	P.M.	P.M.
Perth,	...	...	...	*9 30	*1 0p	4 15	7 30
Stanley Junc	...	...	...	9 55	1 18	4 35	7 55
Murthly,	...	...	...	10 3	...	4 45	8 15
Dunkeld,	...	...	...	10 18	1 40	5 2	8 55
Dalguise,	...	...	...	10 32	...	5 17	9 10
Guay,	...	...	...	10 37	...	5 23	9 20
Ballinluig,	...	...	...	10 45	2 6	5 33	9 30
Pitlochry,	...	...	...	11 0	2 17	5 52	9 45
Blair-Athole	...	...	...	11 20	2 35	6 15	10 10
Struan,	...	...	...	11 35	2 47	...	...
			P.M.				
Dalwhinnie,	...	...	...	12 25	3 32	...	...
			P.M.				
Dalwhinnie,	...	...	12 25	...	4 37	...	...
Struan,	...	...	1 20	...	5 22	...	...
Blair-Athole	7 50	11 30	1 34	...	5 35	...	...
Pitlochry,	8 10	11 47	1 52	...	5 52	...	...
Ballinluig,	8 25	12 0	2 6	...	6 3	...	...
Guay,	8 30	12 7p	2 16	...	...	...	...
Dalguise,	8 35	12 12	2 22	...	6 11	...	...
Dunkeld,	8 50	12 28	2 42	...	6 23	...	...
Murthly,	9 20	12 43	3 0	...	...	...	...
Stanley Junc	9 30	12 50	3 10	...	6 41	...	...
Arrive at							
Perth,	9 50	1 10	3 30	...	7 0	...	...

Excerpt from the timetable revision of 1 December 1863.

Local Goods Trains

Whereas in the early days some local trains were mixed, and the Highland remained a proponent of mixed trains throughout its existence, at Blair Atholl passengers and goods were soon separated into their own services. From then on, there was always just one goods train daily, scheduled such that it left Blair Atholl midmorning shortly before the train from Perth arrived. This was simple common-sense, enabling the small goods yard to be cleared of traffic before another batch appeared only some 20 minutes later. However this did mean that there had to be two locomotives assigned to Blair Atholl's local goods trains. But engines needed to be available twenty-hours a day to assist trains up The Hill, so scheduling two engines from the available 'pool' was easy - the period when the 'pool' would be one engine short was timetabled to occur midmorning between the early morning 'rush' of overnight trains from England and the afternoon sequence of day trains from the south.

Wagons, empty or loaded, that were ready for dispatch south tended to be shunted away from the loading bank and goods shed and into the spare or 'mileage' siding beside the main line. The goods brake van was also parked here – it wasn't needed after its arrival at 10.30am say until departure the next day at 10.00am. Moving wagons about the place wasn't always done conventionally by an engine: man muscle power could be used (I'm not aware that horses were ever used at Blair Atholl, although generally all vehicles had a fixture for tying ropes and this was called a horse-hook). But there were also the techniques of an engine moving wagons on a parallel line, by the engine pulling wagons with a rope and pushing wagons with a wooden pole, both thoroughly risky. I'm not aware that 'pole-shunting' was done at Blair Atholl, but 'rope-shunting' certainly was – special ropes were even supplied by the company for the purpose, and they were tracked, numbered and repaired just like any other company asset. A tow rope was kept in the Goods Shed, although it was supposed to be for emergency use only. The thought of 'pole-shunting' with a long pole jammed at an angle between engine and wagon beggars belief, but 'rope-shunting' seems somewhat less fraught.

As with passengers, variations in goods traffic could be absorbed by putting local goods on through freight trains and, to a lesser extent, through goods on the local. In particular, it was allowed that "a few wagons of coal etc for Blair Atholl" could be carried by any through goods train during the day if required. These trains could be loaded up to 40 wagons. It's not stated whether this coal was destined for the engines or for the local coal merchants, but notorious was the daily Loco Coal Train from Perth to Inverness, a service noted as often requiring three brake vans, so again Blair Atholl received slightly special treatment in order to alleviate problems going over The Hill.

Finally, such traffic as horses and carriages could be loaded onto vehicles that could be hauled by passenger train, so there was always the possibility of having to do this. An example of this is described in the chapter The Loading Gauge. There would always be some disruption of normal routine to shunt these vehicles, but at Blair Atholl an engine or two would typically be on hand to help. In those days, shunting operations were pretty slick, much more so than today – I believe the speed at which shuffling stock around was executed then would surprise most folk today.

The Struan Shuttle

A quirk of the timetable for many years was the service from Blair Atholl to Struan and back. The first local passenger train of the day from Perth, having terminated at Blair Atholl around 7.00am, then shuttled to Struan an hour later only to return yet another hour later ready to depart to Perth. There is no equivalent in the evening, returnees from Blair Atholl availing themselves of a regular passenger train in the early afternoon and evening. Returnees from Struan had Hobson's choice - early afternoon.

Working The Hill

Because of the difficulties of working up The Hill, many trains, especially goods trains, passing through Blair Atholl were subject to special instructions of one sort or another. For example, the 12.40am mixed train, with Sleeping Cars as well as 1st, 2nd and Parliamentary class passengers, was instructed to have a maximum load of 22 goods wagons and no Pilot

LMS Fairburn 2-6-4T No.42169, a latter-day pilot stalwart in BR days, with the crew happily posing, glad to have been interrupted in the very important business of pricking out the fire. (HRS collection)

from Blair Athole. It could haul more to Blair Athole but then had to drop and leave behind the surplus. The 1880 working timetable states that, since 1879, the maximum load for one engine is 24 vehicles up Struan Bank.

The timetables placed restrictions on how much traffic could go over The Hill, and the consequence was that wagons would be removed from trains to wait at Blair Atholl. This is reflected in the provision of two, then three, lay-by sidings northbound. Two overnight through goods trains were scheduled at approximately 4.30am and 6.30am to load up with these wagons to clear Blair Atholl's sidings.

Assisting engines coupled at the front of the train were known as "Pilots", whilst engines pushing trains from the rear were known as "Bankers". The enginemen didn't always follow the rules – in fact the rules were sometimes hair-raisingly flouted. Banking engines would frequently push the rear of the train without being coupled to it – on occasion the main train would get away

BLAIR-ATHOLL.

PILOT ENGINES will be stationed at Blair-Atholl, and assist Down Trains to Dalnaspidal as necessary, returning therefrom to Blair-Atholl as soon after arrival as can be arranged without delaying Train working. Goods Trains worked by Superheated Engines to be confined to single Engine load. Engines of a lower class to have full load, otherwise no assistance to be given.

PILOT ENGINES ASSISTING DOWN GOODS TRAINS FROM BLAIR-ATHOLL.

When a Down Goods Train is assisted from Blair-Atholl, the Assisting Engine must be coupled to the Train, and must push to Dalnaspidal, where it must be detached and there either change to the front of the Train or return to Blair-Atholl as required. It must not be detached from the Train except at a Signal Box. Before starting from Blair-Atholl the Guard must remove his Tail-lamp, and replace it when the Assisting Engine leaves the Train at a Signal Box.

When the Driver of the Engine in front has received the Guard's signal to start from Blair-Atholl, and has satisfied himself that the Line is clear, he must call the attention of the Driver in the rear of the Train by giving him two "Crow" whistles, which must be acknowledged by repetition from the rear Engine, and until these "Crows" have been given and acknowledged, neither the Train Engine nor the Assisting Engine must move forward.

The assisted Train must draw to a stand at Dalnaspidal to detach the rear Engine, and before starting forward the Train must be inspected by the Guard to see that the Couplings have not become uncoupled by the Engine pushing at the rear.

From the Highland Railway's 1922 Working Time Table

from the banker, so deft work was required by the banker's driver to come back into contact with the rear of the train. This had the advantage of course that the banker could simply slip away at the top of The Hill without interrupting the progress of the banked train. The risk here if things went wrong was fairly minimal, but it was another matter altogether when the engine was piloting: pilots would be eased off at the approach to Dalnaspidal, allowing the fireman to clamber to the rear of engine and release the coupling; the driver would go full steam ahead towards the station and, with smart co-operation from the signalman, would run either straight into the parallel running line "wrong line" or continue through the station and reverse back out of the way, all before the main train arrived. These were extremely risky operations in just about every respect; it's a miracle there were no accidents (that we know of) and one wonders whether officialdom in the shape of inspectors ever twigged - there must have been some sort of signal between the men to indicate "don't do it - boss about"!

Bear in mind that for many years, until 1900 in fact, the line was mere single track. Broadly speaking, it could take a goods train one hour fifteen minutes from Blair Atholl to Dalnaspidal. If a train had assistance, the assisting engine would have to return, taking up more time. One could say that up to Dalnaspidal and return could take getting on for two hours. In 1880, there were six timetabled trains each way over Drumochter, plus say four returning assisting engines – a total of sixteen movements. With special trains and an uneven pattern of trains running day and night, it's easy to see how traffic could come to be delayed. And indeed it was.

Basically, the strictures of working The Hill meant that Guards were instructed to leave wagons behind at Blair Atholl to be picked up later by a more lightly loaded train. There was a paragraph on what to do when a coupling might break and thus divide the train in two. If one portion "retrograded" back towards Blair Atholl, when it trundled past Struan, the stationmaster there had to telegraph Blair Atholl *at once* [sic] by Special Message, "in order to admit of the proper arrangements being made in good time to receive it". What those proper

The view behind as No.42169 gets underway with its duties on a sunny day. (HRS collection)

Starting out from Blair Atholl, near Pitagowan.
(HRS collection)

arrangements might have been isn't expressed. However, if there was already a train at Blair Atholl (waiting to leave), and the breakaway was north of Struan, it was instructed that the points at Struan be set to run the train off the rails, in other words to crash it.

All vehicles had brakes of some kind, however crude and ineffective, and all trains had extra braking available under the control of a guard in a brake van. Every goods train between Perth and Inverness had to have a goods brake van in the middle of the train as well as at the rear, and it's been observed that some trains had one at the front as well. Whereas engines were added to trains to assist them up hills, brake vans were needed to control a train going down a hill to prevent the weight of the train overcoming the engine's own meagre brakes.

Such facilities were hardly needed going up The Hill (unless there was a breakaway, when hopefully the guard could prevent "retrogression"). But coming down The Hill was a different matter – at the top, wagon brakes would be pinned down to provide rolling resistance, and the engine and the guard would keep the train under control on the way down. Obviously at the bottom of The Hill, the train's brake would have to be unpinned, and less obviously perhaps, the brake gear allowed to cool down - twenty miles of friction of wood on metal is likely to heat things up somewhat! Thus there were one then two sidings provided at Blair Atholl, one short, one long, so that trains could be held there in preparation for their onward journey. The two southbound lay-by sidings were in use until the 1960s.

The Black Tank

One infamous feature of The Hill is still known as the Black Tank, described by H A Vallance as having an "evil reputation" before the line up The Hill was widened. It was a cutting, narrow, deep and exposed on a sharp left curve, and despite being a cutting was on a hillside, so it could easily fill with snow. The widening of the line reduced the risk somewhat, but even today it is not hard to see the problems that this place caused. It was a cutting through rock, on a curve and of course on the steep gradient, which meant that it was usually slippery, thus providing engines – already working hard getting their trains up to the top – with an even bigger challenge which sometimes would overcome them.

Explanation of the origins of the name Black Tank differ. One is simply that entering the narrow cutting with its vertical granite side, bare and black in the wet, felt like entering a black dank tank.

Another has it that the tank was not a metaphor but was a water-butt at a shepherd's cottage called The Dall in which rain and spring water was collected, his only source of water. The ruin of this cottage can be seen on the hillside across from the A9. This house was occupied by a shepherd and his family very many years ago. The shepherd's widow (who by then resided in Glen Fender, Blair Atholl) told of how the firemen of the passing engines would throw out coal for her use – if no coal was thrown, she knew an inspector was on the train!

When snow is being blown sideways in a wind, any depression in the ground reduces the air pressure above it and the snow has a tendency to simply drop into the depression, thus filling it. When the depression is a deep cutting the same thing happens, with the inevitable result of a good deep snow blockage. This same property was actually used to the railway's advantage with their snow fences – these were like large picket fences using old sleepers instead of palings, strongly braced and set some way back from the railway line. They didn't get blown over because of the gaps between sleepers, but the wind whistling over and through resulted in low pressure on the leeward side of the fence and caused the snow to quietly drop beside the fence rather than on the railway itself. Sometimes there would be two of three rows of such snow fences. Their remains can still be seen in places - often sculpted into strange shapes by wind and rain rather than simply rotted away. These fences were not on railway land, but the adjacent landowners never seemed to mind (or charge), perhaps seeing them

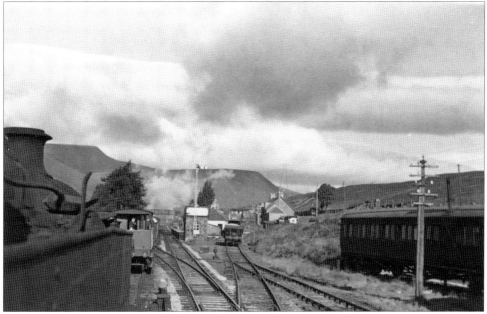

Slipping away at Dalnaspidal. The train will continue on its way without stopping – the signal which can just be made out under the footbridge is 'off', giving the right of way. The banker will reverse through the crossover in the foreground. If necessary, it can replenish from the water tank, and wait in the siding off to the right until time to go down the hill back to Blair Atholl. Water was loaded into the engine's tanks by means of a long tarpaulin bag by pulling a long chain to a valve in the tank; these bags were latterly replaced by canvas bags. Dalnaspidal was notorious as one of the coldest spots on the system, and not only did the water freeze but the bags froze too. Tarpaulin could withstand the conditions better than canvas which damaged easily - when frozen solid they would break rather than bend. A stock of spare bags was kept in Blair Atholl's shed for that very reason. (HRS collection)

Looking northward inside the infamous Black Tank. The track is steep and sharp; being on the side of a hill, snow could fill this entire cutting, all the more so when there was just a single track carving through the rock.
(Howard Geddes)

as not only being of benefit to the railway but also advantageous to themselves in terms of windbreaks and shelter.

Beside the Black Tank is a terrace of three cottages, now extremely ruinous. Until a year or two ago there was an access footbridge from the road across the river – even this has now collapsed making The Black Tank effectively inaccessible. These cottages were built by the railway for their permanent way workers who were responsible for maintaining this section of line. Such dwellings had to be provided every few miles, some built new by the railway and some taken over from tradespeople who owed their living to road traffic soon to be superseded by the railway. Many of these dwellings were in bleak spots along the line, but, with the Black Tank's reputation, the cottages there on the east flank of the hill could hardly be surpassed for an inhospitable location in winter.

The Shopping Train

Speaking of these remote cottages, there was an unusual train service that served these cottages. This was an employees-only passenger train, known as the Housewife's Choice (after a radio programme of the time) which went from Blair Atholl north to Kingussie on alternate Saturdays, stopping whenever required at any of the railwaymen's cottages along the line to pick up the womenfolk, for shopping in Kingussie. In 1951 its official description was "Conveys workmen and families to and from Kingussie for provisions" and it was to call at Black Tank, Dalanraoch, County March, Balsporran, Inchlea. [Ref: British Railways Magazine, London Midland Region, August, 1951]

The train had but a single carriage. At one time, all the odder, both the engine and coach started from Perth by hitching a lift with a normal local passenger train. The two vehicles unhitched themselves at Blair Atholl to form the Housewife's Choice thence departing northwards on its shopping expedition. The disposal of the train (to the north or return to the south) is shrouded in mystery; the coach probably returned in what was known as a Stock Train – one such departed Inverness at 2.20am hauling empty coaching stock in order to reposition vehicles involved in unbalanced workings, which was most prevalent in the summer when the traffic was 'peaky'. The laden shoppers were left to their own devices too. I haven't come across any reference to the special train's return and only assume that their return was effected by hitching lifts in the brake vans of southbound goods trains, scheduled passenger trains hardly being allowed to stop at a bare lineside upon request.

The Final Trip Home

In 1902 Her Grace, Louisa, Duchess of Atholl, suffering from poor health, travelled to Italy with her husband and daughter in the hope that the Mediterranean climate would be of benefit to her. The Duke was required to return home in order to attend the Coronation of King Edward VII which was due to take place on 26th June 1902, but the ceremony had to be postponed because the King developed appendicitis (eventually taking place on 9th August 1902), so the Duke remained in Britain awaiting royal developments.

On 8th July 1902, whilst travelling by train from Italy to Switzerland, the Duchess took a turn for the worse and unfortunately died. The Duke, summoned by Telegram, immediately rushed to the Continent, only to then return to Scotland with his daughter to make the funeral arrangements. The Duchess's body came home separately, accompanied on the journey by the family's physician, Dr. Anderson. Illustrated here is the counterfoil of the Great Northern Railway Ticket, made out in Dr. Anderson's name, dated 15th July 1902, for the carriage of the corpse from King's Cross to Blair Atholl at the cost of £23.13s.0d.

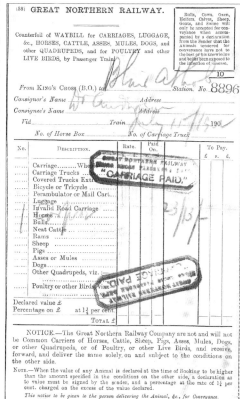

(John Roake collection)

The *Perthshire Advertiser* takes up the story:-

The remains of the late Duchess of Atholl arrived at Blair Atholl yesterday by the 10.45 train from Perth. On arriving at the station the van containing the coffin was promptly shunted on to the 'up line' by a special engine which the railway officials had in readiness. Upon the van being brought opposite the Castle private waiting room, the coffin was taken in charge by Mr. Forbes, Old Blair, and Dr. Anderson. From the van it was transferred to the 'waiting room' and thence to the hearse, which Mr. Winton, Pitlochry, had in waiting outside the station buildings. The hearse was then slowly drawn up the Avenue to the Castle, arriving there about one o'clock.

Despite the macabre use in this instance of a ticket intended for live animals, carriage of corpses in coffins was a common service provided by the railways, indeed some railways even had specialised Corpse Vans and the London Necropolis Railway had dedicated facilities at Waterloo for funeral trains bound for the Necropolis at Brookwood (and must have been the only railway company with a skull and crossbones as its coat of arms).

A typical view, taken in LMS times. On the right, the original waiting shed survives; but not for much longer. The chimneys were unstable and troublesome even from the earliest days: the one teetering shows it's about to be replaced by the shed that is there today. In the far distance the Old Mill Garage building with its tall chimney seems to be in use at this time as a bakehouse. (Author's collection)

Going up: LMS designed Fairburn 2-6-4T No. 42169 setting off up The Hill in a flurry of steam, ready for a hard slog for nearly 16 miles to Dalnaspidal, the Summit being yet a further two miles. The push starts straightaway to get the train underway, and is relentless. (HRS collection)

Up and Down

Traffic on the Highland Railway expanded continuously over the years. The HR's own system was extending, with lines to Thurso, Wick and Kyle. And the Victorian love affair with the romantic Highlands meant much increased traffic from the south, one of the consequences being the arrival of heavy sleeping cars and Pullman cars, with well-off families travelling in their private saloons accompanied by ancillary luggage vans, horseboxes, carriage trucks, and staff. The Glorious Twelfth usually resulted in inglorious delays as the mad rush north converged on Perth to make its way through Blair Atholl and over The Hill. Single-track working is bad enough, but single-track working up and down The Hill was exceptionally difficult. By the end of the 1880s it had become clear that the bottleneck was such that doubling of the track was the only solution.

In 1892, a major plan was proposed, doubling the track from Stanley Junction through Blair Atholl and up The Hill. Plans at Blair Atholl show that Tilt Viaduct was to be doubled - I suspect in much the same way that the bridge at Calvine was extended, namely by building a new bridge alongside the existing. The doubled track would sweep round to join the existing loop beside the platforms, and thence onwards towards Struan. The engine shed was to be greatly expanded – doubled in size by doubling either its length or width; I shouldn't think tripling it by doing both despite both extensions being shown on the plan. Doubling its width, with two new approach roads unable to be fitted into the available space, meant the bridge over the Banvie Burn would need widening: this might have been the thinking behind the alternative of extending the shed lengthways. This doubling all the way from Perth was turned down on financial grounds.

A revised plan dated October 1892 was presented which shows that doubling south of Blair Atholl has been abandoned; instead the station loop is lengthened as far as it could go towards the Tilt Viaduct. The rising embankment west of the Banvie Burn is to be widened to the north to take the second line of rails: this results in an awkward slew to the right because the new southbound track is not in line with the bridge over the Banvie Burn. The logic is clear enough on the plan, but it's hardly elegant. Perhaps the most surprising aspect of the plan is that the southbound platform is extended to over double its present length by building it right up to the Banvie Burn, thus making it even longer than the current northbound platform (where there was unquestionably no room to extend it any more without a complete rebuild of all the northbound side). This extension meant that the goods yard had to be redesigned: the Goods Shed stayed where it was but the mileage siding and the southbound lay-by siding were merged into one siding which turned off the main line on the east side of the Banvie Burn; this in turn meant the Banvie Burn bridge had now to be expanded even more to cope with a fourth track. The goods shed was now accessed by the erstwhile loading bank siding which came off this new lay-by siding over Banvie Burn. The layout changes, leading to a diminution of siding and goods facilities, simply to achieve a lengthened southbound platform, were clearly way out of hand. Not surprisingly common-sense prevailed and both aspects of the plan that would require a widening of the Banvie Burn bridge – the lengthening of the platform and the conversion of the engine shed from two roads to four roads – never happened.

In the event, this proposal was also rejected in its entirety, but matters were pressing.

Dormitory at Blair Atholl. This dormitory has been specially fitted up for the benefit of Enginemen and Firemen who may be stationed at Blair Atholl as spare men : and will also be for the use of Enginemen and Firemen arriving at Blair Atholl and having time to rest themselves but not having sufficient time at their disposal to look for lodging elsewhere.

It must be distinctly under-stood that the Dormitory will be used solely as a bedroom for the benefit of those requiring it, and as such must be kept clean as circumstance will permit.

It will be under the charge of the Loco. Foreman and will be locked up when not in use.

Should any damage be done to any portion thereof by any of the occupants during his stay he will be held responsible for the cost of repairs. (David Jones Loco. Supt. 26 March 1894)

I don't think this is simply an improvement for improvement's sake. Instead I infer a worsening situation at Blair Atholl with delays, sometimes lengthy, requiring more than a mess but less than lodging. The Dormitory building became the Old Mill Garage.

The need to double the line became ever more pressing. And eventually, on 6 August 1897, powers were obtained to execute the doubling of the line. Blair Atholl came under Contract No.1 (Struan Contract) which started at the north points of the station loop at precisely 35 miles 3,117 feet from Perth and included a new Garry Viaduct at Struan. In contrast to the 1892 plans, the track changes at Blair Atholl were confined to the north end and essentially comprised extending the northbound loop, this time with a sensible realignment over the Banvie Burn bridge to achieve a smooth transition from station loop to double track main line. The only other impact on Blair Atholl itself was that it was where materials and equipment for the contract were offloaded and stored. Dated 1 January 1898, and signed on 23 June 1898 and 12 July 1898 by the contractor John Best, Edinburgh, completion for this section was specified as 15 March 1900.

The expansion of the loco shed and associated sidings started in earnest, even before the widening commenced, with requisite land being purchased from the Duke of Atholl in various dribs and drabs during 1898 and 1899. One of the plans that show this activity also shows a second Tilt Viaduct to the south of the existing one, and of identical design, associated with a piece of land only 0.08 of an acre to be acquired. This is clearly in connection with line doubling to Perth. The plan, however, is a proposal for acquisition in July 1900, totalling 1½ acres, and never came to fruition. But the intention of having two Tilt Viaducts side by side is intriguing. The time limit for doubling the whole line, including south of Blair Atholl over the River Tilt, was repeatedly extended until 1938, so even until then there remained the possibility of huge change to the village's view of the railway over the river.

To help the contractors meet even an agreed revised date of 1 July 1900 (the HR having first demanded the date be brought forward to 1 March 1900), the HR put in special service sidings near Dalnaspidal and the Black Tank "for providing convenience for the conveyance of

Shown as the dormitory on a 1901 plan of nearby land acquired by the HR, this building is said to have been a bakehouse, in later years becoming the Old Mill Garage and now converted for self-catering. But the 1892 line-doubling proposal (which shows all buildings) does not show this building, so I conclude that the building was new in 1894, becoming a bakehouse when its use as a dormitory was superseded, later finding a new use as a garage for the motor-car. (Author)

material". The contractor had wanted to work his trains on the "open line". This thoroughly dangerous-sounding idea was countered by the HR agreeing to run a special train "during pleasure" between Blair Atholl and Dalnaspidal for the contractor's convenience (whatever that means - just whose pleasure isn't clear!). It was reported on 1 August 1899 that 478 men were at work. The widened track was opened 2 July 1900 to Dalnacardoch Signal Cabin, 13 May 1901 to Dalnaspidal, 10 June 1901 to the County March at the summit. One of the reasons the contractor gave for the delays was that the HR treated the Pilot Engine as a Train all the way from Blair Atholl up to Dalnaspidal and back again causing long delays to the contractor waiting for line time. Claims continued to be made by affected landowners to the HR for such things as damage to a timber bridge over the Garry at the Black Tank and land being taken from the Glebe. On 6 November 1901, John Robertson of Old Blair on behalf of the Duke complained "These cottages now being erected and their sequel are to spoil a pretty village". He didn't mention that the previous year he had already sold 2½ acres to the HR for the express purpose of building those houses, intended for the railwaymen needed for the enhanced facilities.

A rather odd arrangement was detailed in October 1900 when the HR declared that the railway land taken for the line widening included 18" outside the railway fence, the area for each tenant affected up to Balnacroft being precisely calculated. This same arrangement is explicitly drawn on the 1892 proposals, showing the railway fence in cross-section actually part way up the slope of the embankment, and there is no mention of drainage ditches. Quite what was achieved by allowing tenants free access to farm the bottom slope of the embankment isn't at all clear.

The workmen's houses complained about were built during 1901 as a block of four, being the extant block of two facing Garryside; at the same time the block of six cottages by the goods shed were converted into three. Alex Cattenach was the main builder, with William Duncan

Coming down: After steam, Sultzer diesels Class 24s and 26s were the mainstay over the Highland lines, often two coupled together and even three on occasion. Class 24 D5119 arrives from the north down The Hill and over the Banvie Burn bridge. Note the "laddered" points over the bridge – the exit from the engine shed couldn't have been squeezed any further: an indication of how the Banvie Burn so constrained the track layout at Blair Atholl. Note the signal allowing the train to enter Blair Atholl is on the "wrong" side of the track. *(HRS collection)*

carpenter, both local men, the buildings being completed and paid for without any fuss.

The station was taking on its fully developed look. Mention must be made of the gents urinals provided towards the end of the northbound platform, presumably more for the convenience of the engine crew than passengers. Whilst the engine was being watered, so the opposite for its crew.... By 1902 the entire so-called Tulloch Estate was acquired and the modern boundaries of railway property were achieved. The Duke's lime trees that had lined the boundary stone wall all the way along the south side of the station since the 1860s were now in the way of expansion; they seem to have been cut down in 1902 with compensation being paid to the Duke shortly after November 1902. The loco yard expanded a bit more to its final layout.

The doubled mainline was extended a few years later: 1 June 1908 to Balsporran and 17 May 1909 to Dalwhinnie. Thus Blair Atholl station served its eponymous village and surrounding neighbourhood, and the engine shed provided the engines and men to assist heavy trains up The Hill for many years, in fact until the end of the 1950s. By this time, the end of steam was nigh; diesel multiple units replaced steam on the Blair Atholl locals on 15 June 1959. With diesel engines taking over all duties and the railway service declining overall, there was no longer any need for banking and bankers. Heavy trains were hauled throughout by two or even three diesel engines. In 1962 the engine shed formally closed and not long afterwards the track was lifted for scrap, with some other materials also recovered for scrap, like the water tanks and the turntable. A desolate sweep of cinders was left behind with the water tank bases and the loco shed isolated and empty; the turntable pit yawning.

The lay-by sidings remained, as did the goods yard. But first the local passenger service was withdrawn 3 April 1965 and then the goods service ended 7 November 1966. During that summer of 1966 the track up The Hill was singled, leaving the two lines through the station between the two signal boxes still operated as double-track. On 25 August 1968 the last vestige of double-track operation ended with the closure of Blair Atholl North signal box, and although the loop through the station remained the whole of the old Highland main line up from the south through Blair

The Modern Image: EWS 67004 on a DHL parcels train waits for First Direct's 'Turbostar' 170396 to arrive from Perth on a stopping passenger train for Inverness in September 2006.   (Howard Geddes)

Tilt Viaduct, the original structure, now reinforced, in 2009 (Keith Fenwick)

Atholl over The Hill was once again single line. Even the station building was subject to cuts – as described on page 69 the east wing had to be amputated before it collapsed.

But these were cuts too far, for the oil boom had come about, and, having expensively singled the line, even more expensively the line was redoubled, reopening on 24 April 1978.

By now Blair Atholl was reduced to being only another station on the Perth to Inverness main line. Its importance and individuality as a railway centre, which had made it worthy of study in its own right in a book such as this, had dissipated, even though some sidings lingered on for railway maintenance purposes. Its subsequent history is essentially no more than the history of the ex-Highland Railway's main line, and this can be, and will be, better told by others.

Suffice to say here that the future of Blair Atholl as a passenger station seems assured; even an occasional assessment occurs looking into the prospects of reintroducing freight exploiting the land still available albeit overgrown. And there are substantial reminders of the old days. While the old engine shed still exists, serving a useful purpose, it's only realistic to consider how it can have a permanent future. Much the same has to be said even about the station building in its lopsided condition. It is a minor miracle that the signal box by the level crossing still exists, needed to control the semaphore signals which themselves linger on worked in the traditional method. Indeed, their survival has more than a little to do with the inordinate time and cost it takes these days to provide the simplest of new facilities; in the long meantime, delight in the creak of the signal wires and the bouncing clonk of the signal arm by the level crossing, shaking the very post that supports it, the same as has happened for over a century.

All other original features have either been replaced or buried under later improvements - the Banvie Burn bridge, the platforms, even the insignificant yet essential culverts carrying the mill stream - all gone or changed out of all recognition.

Yet one object does survive: the Tilt Viaduct, even though bolstered and strengthened, is magnificent for being probably the only original feature of the railway at Blair Atholl still in full use. Built for the opening of the railway in 1863 and as much part of the village scene as the station ever was, it stands as a monument to the skill and passion of Joseph Mitchell in building the railway over the mountains and thus shaping Blair Atholl as a Highland Railway village.

HR No.1 Ben-y-Gloe: still in HR livery, after the Great War, the loco is posed in front of the water tanks alongside the engine shed. (Atholl Country Life Museum)

Standing, left to right:
1. Willie Bain, gaffer
2. Tommy Bain
3. M McRobert
4. Kenny Munro
5. John Sutherland
6. same person as photo on page 56, backrow-8
7. Bob Ireland
8. John McGillvary

On footplate, left to right:
1. Bob Simpson
2. Kenny Grant
3. Tom Bruce, fitter
4. same person as photo on page 56, frontrow-8
5. Davie Burnet, driver
6. Danny Smith, fireman
7. Jim McKenzie
8. Hugh McIntosh
9. Alex Murdoch

MEN AND MACHINE

An Army marches on its stomach, so it is said. In the same way, so does the Iron Horse, requiring to be fed with coal and water at frequent intervals. But the suppliers of this sustenance are the men of the railway, and there was quite a community at Blair Atholl. It has also been said that many of the original Irish navvies who built the railway stayed on, but I have not seen any actual evidence either that the navvies were predominantly Irish or that they stayed on, although I must admit I haven't looked very deeply so I could very well be mistaken. Instead the censuses show a typical mix of inhabitants. Most of those employed by the railway occupied cottages provided by the HR their employers, whilst nearly all the others were boarders or lodgers (I interpret boarders as being long-term and lodgers short-term guests of the host family). I have tried to discover every railway employee in the village: they all lived in the immediate locality of Blair Atholl station, if not in the station cottages themselves then in Garryside. Some might have slipped through the net, away working, although I have discovered only one family where the husband was explicitly absent.

Census:	1871	1881	1891	1901
Total	17	25	27	35
of whom				
Drivers	2	4	3	6
Stokers/Firemen	1	4	5	5
Pointsmen/Signalmen	3	2	4	5
Guards	1	1	1	1

The censuses reflect the increase in employment over the decades, the doubling of the line clearly having an effect. Over the period in the table, there seems to have only ever been one guard. The timetables show that at least one of the local passenger trains always lay overnight at Blair Atholl, thus reasonably accounting for a guard permanently based at Blair Atholl. But this implies that the staffing arrangements for the daily goods train, with its departure on any one day to Perth a few minutes before the day's arrival from Perth, were more complex than at first appear.

The 1871 and 1881 census show four cottages in the goods yard, just as expected. The 1891 census lists seven station cottages rather than the eight there were in reality: the cottage of Donald M'Gregor must have been empty: being a surfaceman maybe he was out on the line and slipped past the census enumerator. In 1901 there are now ten cottages in the goods yard plus the cottages beside the railway crossing, all occupied by railwaymen. At least 35 people living just around the station were employed on the railway, supporting their families. The 1911 census shows the effect of six cottages being converted to three, seven cottages being recorded in 1911 instead of ten in 1901.

The censuses are more fully laid out at the end of this chapter; I have noted who were there for long periods, namely those who appeared in two consecutive censuses – this is not an infallible indication of continuity of railway employment in a family, because the mantle might have passed from father to son. We are fortunate that a series of Valuation Rolls are accessible. These range annually from 1885/86 to 1898/99, and show the occupiers of every dwelling including those owned by the HR. Whilst lodgers and boarders are not listed, they show each year who was occupying each of the HR's dwellings in the goods yard. One of the cottages was slightly bigger and more prestigious than the rest (it had five rooms with windows whereas the

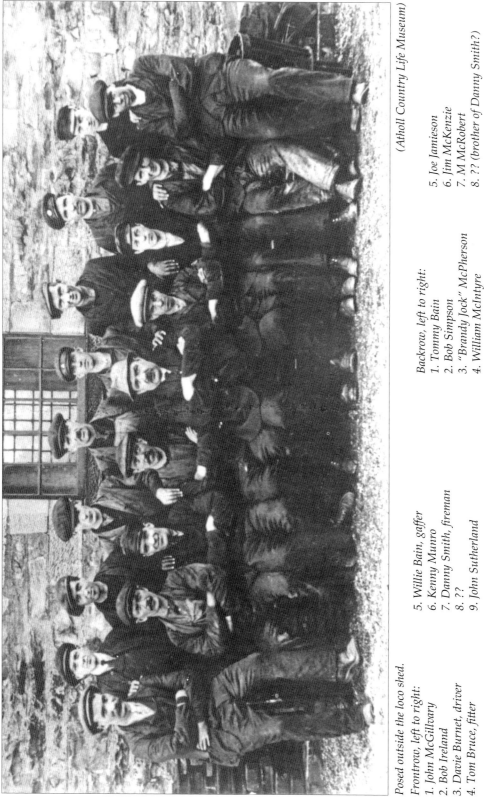

Posed outside the loco shed. (Atholl Country Life Museum)

Front row, left to right:
1. John McGillvary
2. Bob Ireland
3. Davie Burnet, driver
4. Tom Bruce, fitter
5. Willie Bain, gaffer
6. Kenny Munro
7. Danny Smith, fireman
8. ??
9. John Sutherland

Back row, left to right:
1. Tommy Bain
2. Bob Simpson
3. "Brandy Jock" McPherson
4. William McIntyre
5. Joe Jamieson
6. Jim McKenzie
7. M McRobert
8. ?? (brother of Danny Smith?)

others had four – a metric recorded in the censuses). Occupied by the Gaffer, his was valued at £6pa whereas everyone else's was £4pa – the HR paid these amounts, not the occupiers. Details of one of the Valuation Rolls is listed; the others are too repetitive to warrant inclusion.

The gaffer in 1881 was Alexander Campbell who had been an Engine Foreman at Kilmarnock. It's not known whether he was the first of such position at Blair Atholl, but it is possible. Certainly there didn't seem to be such a person in 1871. He moved on and died in Forres in 1885. By 1885, Alexander Clark was Locomotive Foreman, apparently coming into the railway ranks in conventional manner, having been a blacksmith in Middle Ardo, Belhelvie in 1871, then aged 24. In 1894, he was promoted to Locomotive Works Foreman at Inverness. Before the new line over Slochd was built and Aviemore grew in railway importance, it appears that Blair Atholl was the main significant station between Perth and Inverness, even more so than Forres or Elgin. Thus promotion from Blair Atholl could lead to a position at Inverness, whereas in later years Aviemore became the next level up.

A couple of incidents which occurred during Clark's regime are recorded:

John MacLachlan, Driver, and James Begbie, Fireman, are fined 2/6 each for neglecting to fill their tender tank with water before leaving Blair Atholl on 1st inst, in consequence of which they had to drop off the 7.5am down train which they were assisting – 8 September 1891. (Both these men lived in the Station Cottages at Blair Atholl.)

The 9.50am up Special train of 27th ult was booked to cross the 11.50am down train at Blair Atholl but owing to the enginemen not keeping the former under proper control it overshot the starting signal which was standing at danger and was only pulled up outside the south Main Line crossing, and for this carelessness Donald Macintosh and Alex. Sim are each fined 1/- – 3-2-1892.

Alexander Clark's replacement, from 1894, was William Gall Barclay, who entitled himself Locomotive Engineer in the 1901 census. He had ideas literally above his station: he was the son of John Brown Barclay who was the younger brother of William Barclay, the first Superintendent of the Line from 1855 to 1865; the story of elder brother William Barclay's flawed career with the I&AJR, eventually being dismissed for fishing when he should have been superintending, has been told elsewhere, but we may note here that it was under his auspices that the first batches of engines were

Donald Fraser, Stationmaster 1898-1928. The footbridge over the line had its normal lattice work on the steps filled in, on the explicit orders of the Duke, so that no one standing underneath would be able to determine just how true a Scotsman he was when he climbed the bridge in his kilt. There was also a modesty-board on the sides of the footbridge. Photos show the set up during Highland days, but they seem to have been removed very early in LMS days: there in 1925, gone by 1930.

(Authors' collection)

introduced and which so struggled over The Hill when the line opened. We may also note that John Brown Barclay, having entered railway service with the Inverness & Nairn in 1855, was in charge of running the I&AJR trains between Perth and Pitlochry when the Perth & Dunkeld line was extended to Pitlochry in May 1863; therefore, he will have been a key figure in the logistics of building the line through Blair Atholl. When William G Barclay married a second time in December 1896, he promoted himself to be Railway Locomotive Superintendent, a deception that would not have been appreciated, had he been found out, by the real Superintendent, Peter Drummond, who had just taken office the previous month. His father by now was himself still at Inverness; he had moved there in the 1860s and had succeeded David Jones as Locomotive Works Foreman when the latter became Locomotive Superintendent in 1870. William G Barclay was still at Blair Atholl in 1911 in his cottage, self-designated Loco Superintendent. He moved to St Rollox, and died outwith the district in 1941 age 75.

His successor was William Gault who in 1901 had been a Locomotive Fitter under William G Barclay; at that time, Willie Gault lived in one of the cottages by the level crossing, a boarder in the McGregor household. Bearing in mind that today's cottage used to be two dwellings, widow Mary McGregor looked after grown-up sons Donald (28) and Alexander (24) as well as two boarders (age 29 and 38), not forgetting a grandson. Next door one way was even more cosy: Kenneth Munro had a wife and a family of four, plus five lodgers. Next door the other way, the Rosses were a family of 11, but they managed with only one boarder. In those four dwellings, nowadays two cottages, there were 35 people living and working.

We may assume that Willie Gault moved into the gaffer's cottage. After a relatively short tenure, in 1916 Willie Gault moved to Aviemore, where his subsequent career is well documented.

A later gaffer was Willie Bain, for ten years from about 1920 to 1930. Very approximately around 1923, he and his men posed for a couple of splendid photographs in the company of Blair Atholl's adopted engine No. 1 *Ben-y-Gloe*, allocated to Blair Atholl for local passenger trains to Perth. The accompanying photos shows the throng assembled; best efforts have been made to identify everyone.

If the Gaffer was no mean force to be reckoned with in keeping his engines in good fettle, the Station Master (or Agent as the Highland tended to call them) was indeed the master of all, managing the business of the station. The title Agent is not misleading: they did have a responsibility for bringing business to the railway. For the present, I can only glean their names from the censuses. But they were all in post for quite lengthy periods, so it's possible there were no others. I can only give approximate dates.

1863-1873 approx: Charles James Dunn was station master in 1871. Born in Montrose in 1838, he was a railway clerk in Montrose in 1861. But when he married in October 1864 at Blairgowrie, he was already Station Master at Blair Atholl. This means it is very likely

Inside Blair-Atholl South in more modern times with a train leaving under the control of Marcel Graham, with an unknown visitor. (Author's collection)

he came to Blair Athole as Station Master for the opening of the railway. He was still there in 1872 but by 1874 the family were in Glasgow when he opened a pub in Carrick St called the Montrose Bar where he was licensee until 1907, followed by his daughter until 1937. The Gas Works in Blair Atholl came into operation in 1871; in their records, a certain C J Dunn required payment for the period from July 1871 to October 1872 of £4-1-10 for Fireclay and £157-16-3d for Coal and Cartage. Interesting that this was in his own name and not that of the railway: he was thus the first coal merchant. This would be recurring business, far exceeding any other expenses, with only a one-off payment of £130-10-1 matching it, to James Macdonald for fitting up Blair and Garryside with piping and gas fittings. In later years, John Campbell supplied the coal, at a rate of around £200 pa.

1873-1885 say: David Henderson, who was born in Foveran, son of a farmer, but joined the railway as a Porter and was in Dunkeld by 1861. By 1871 he was a Guard based in Perth. By 1876 he is at Blair Atholl, presumably now as Station Master, or Railway Agent as was the usual title then in vogue; his son William is an engine cleaner. And in 1881 he is recorded as the Station Master. But then I lose track of him after 1881.

By 1891 - 1898: Duncan McLennan (was still at Blair Atholl in 1895 where and when his son was born). Born 1856 at Contin in Ross-shire, he doesn't seem to have joined the railway until after 1881 when he was a carpenter in Inverness. He must have risen the ranks rapidly to become the stationmaster at Blair Athole in 1891. He moved on, and in 1901 he turns up in Athole Cottage, Fodderty, as the Station Agent. He died 1 May 1925 and on his gravestone in Garve kirkyard he is commemorated as Stationmaster, Dornoch.

1898 - 1928: Donald Fraser (stated by a descendant to have been stationmaster from 1898 to 1928, he must have taken over from Duncan McLellan). Born 1861, he came from Kirkhill, six miles west of Inverness near Beauly. In 1891 he was stationmaster at Achterneed, starting out his career as a railway clerk at Stromeferry. In 1901 and again in 1911 he is recorded at Blair Atholl.

14397 Ben-y-Gloe *about to depart with a relief train to Perth on 4 August 1939. The poster on the newspaper kiosk announces "Welcome Back Gracie" – had Gracie Fields just returned from a foreign tour?* *(DLGH Hunter / HRS collection)*

Surviving staff records are very incomplete, so one can only take a peek at what there is and not assume this is anywhere near a complete picture. Judging by the censuses and the valuation rolls, the details below are definitely sparse, although at least we can say that there are now two guards in town.

Staff at Blair Atholl at end of 1911:

Donald Fraser	Stationmaster	Joined	1-4-1877 as clerk at Dingwall
salary 1-10-1910 : £105			
William Thomson	Booking clerk	Joined	23-2-1903 as Clerk at Burghead
salary 1-10-1911 : £55		Left	28-3-1912 "own accord"
Edward Kemp	Goods clerk	Joined	1-11-1905 as Clerk at Forres
salary 1-10-1911 : £50		Moved	31-7-1912 to Dunkeld
Alexander Cruickshank	Guard	Joined	30-4-1900
		Promoted	13-5-1913 to Passenger Guard
James MacKenzie	Guard	Joined	8-2-1909
		Promoted	13-5-1913 to Passenger Guard
James McQueen	Nightman		
John Jamieson	Foreman		
John Ross	Gatekeeper		
Alexander McIntosh	Pointsman	Promoted	25-11-1912 to Signalman Blair Atholl
James Forbes	Pointsman		
Alexander Smith	Porter		
Mrs Ross	Office Cleaner	(ever since 1883)	
Mrs MacKenzie	Gatekeeper	King's Island Gates (towards Killiecrankie)	

Some others who joined during 1912:

Alistair Chisholm	Booking clerk	Joined	28-3-1912
salary 28-3-1912 : £50		Left	9-11-1912
Angus McDonald	Booking clerk	Joined	8-11-1912
salary 8-11-1912 : £55		Left	2-6-1917 for military service
David Sutherland	Porter	Period	8-7-1912 to 25-9-1912
James Baigrie	Porter	Period	5-8-1912 to 30-9-1912
George Smith	Signalman	From	1-7-1912
	Pointsman	From	4-9-1912 (suggests a demotion)

Others who had spells at Blair Atholl:

I am unclear why the three porters below are not listed under those at Blair Atholl at end 1911.

Donald McIntyre	8-6-1904	Porter, Blair Atholl	15/- pw
	20-7-1914	Foreman Porter, Dunkeld	22/- pw
Alexander Bartlett	27-5-1907	Porter, Blair Atholl	15/- pw
	24-6-1912	Nightman, Moulinearn	22/6 pw
	24-7-1912	Day Pointsman, Moulinearn	21/- pw
	28-10-1912	Spare, Inverness	
John Doig	1-7-1908	Porter, Blair Atholl	15/- pw
	24-6-1912	Nightman, Inchmagranachan	21/6 pw
	7-10-1917	Spare, Inverness	
John McLennan	14-6-1909	Porter, Blair Atholl	15/- pw
	9-4-1911	Porter, Pitlochry	17/- pw
	28-2-1912	Pointsman, Nairn	
	29-7-1912	Pointsman, Dunkeld	19/- pw
	5-10-1912	Absent & drinking	Paid off
	31-1-1913	Given another chance: to Kyle as Porter	

George Anderson	26-8-1912	Joined as Porter, Hopeman	
	13-7-1914	to Moulinearn	
	17-8-1914	to Blair Atholl	
Alexander Scott	1-12-1913	Joined as Messenger, Perth	
	later	to Aberfeldy	
	19-10-1917	to Army	
	9-2-1919	to Blair Atholl, having returned from Army	
Donald Wilson	21-3-1916	Learner Clerk, Blair Atholl	6/- pw
	3-7-1916	Clerk, Killiecrankie	£20pa
	3-7-1917	Clerk, Killiecrankie	£25pa

Blair-Atholl North, on a peaceful day; Signalman Graham taking the air. While I was there not one train came through, such was the lack of service in 1963.
(Howard Geddes)

Inside Blair Atholl south. Every boy's dream! That boy, though, isn't me.
(Author's collection)

Railway Employees : 1871 census

Name	Address	Job**	Ref*
Charles Dunn	Blair Atholl	Railway Station Agent	7-13-15
Duncan Mcpherson	Blair Atholl	Railway Carriage Inspector	7-14-21
David Murray	Blair Atholl	Railway Pointsman	7-15-1
James Mackintosh	Blair Atholl	Telegraph Lineman	7-16-5
James Riach	Blair Atholl	Railway Pointsman	7-17-8
John Christie	Lanark Cottage boarder	Railway Stoker	7-21-9
Mr Ferguson	Garryside	Engine Driver	7-26-10
George Mcrae	Garryside boarder	Railway Pointsman	7-26-14
James Nicoll	Garryside boarder	Railway Engine Cleaner	7-26-15
Donald Mcintosh	Garryside boarder	Railway Engine Cleaner	7-26-16
James Insch	Garryside boarder	Railway Porter	7-26-17
Peter Stewart	Garryside	Railway Guard	7-27-18
Hugh Mcgregor	Garryside lodger	Railway Clerk	7-29-11
Robert Henderson	Garryside	Railway Engine Driver	7-33-4
John Hattle	Garryside	Engine Driver	7-34-9
Duncan Clark	Garryside boarder	Railway Clerk	7-37-12
Hugh Cameron	Old Blair	Surfaceman	7-57-21

* Ref: Enumeration District 7 covered Blair Atholl village, including the station, Garryside and Blair Castle. The next number (for us, the most important) is that assigned to one household by the census enumerator; the final number shows the row on the census return itself.

**Job is exactly as recorded in the census.

Small Ben No.1 **Ben-y-Gloe** *on the turntable, in the striking crimson red of LMS passenger engines. The open urinal on the platform is in the background (probably just as well).*   *(HRS collection)*

Railway Employees : 1881 census

Name	Address	Job	Ref	1871?
William Sutherland	Blair village lodger	Engine Fireman	7-5a-5	
John Murray	Blair village lodger	Ry Engine Driver	7-5b-6	
John Fraser	Blair village	Ry Pointsman	7-11-5	
John Murdoch	Blair village lodger	Ry Engine Cleaner	7-11a-7	
John MacKintosh	Blair village lodger	Ry Porter	7-11b-8	
John Mcgregor	Railway Crossing	Ry Surfaceman	7-12-9	
David Henderson	Rly Station House	Ry Agent	7-13-1	
William H Henderson	Rly Stn House son	Ry Engine Cleaner	7-13-3	
Alexander Campbell	Station Cottages	Ry Loco Foreman	7-14-11	
David Small	Station Cottages	Ry Pointsman	7-15-19	
James Sutherland	Stn Cottages lodger	Ry Clerk	7-15a-25	
William Begbie	Station Cottages	Ry Carriage Inspector	7-16-1	
Peter Brown	Stn Cottages lodger	Telegraph Lineman	7-16a-6	
John Calder *	Station Cottages	Engine Driver	7-17-7	
John McLachlan	Garryside	Ry Engine Fireman	7-19a-1	
William Dargavel	Garryside	Ry Engine Driver	7-20-2	
William Dargavel	Garryside son	Ry Engine Cleaner	7-20-4	
Peter Stewart	Garryside	Ry Guard	7-21-11	Yes
Donald Junor	Garryside lodger	Ry Engine Driver	7-23a-13	
John Ritchie	Garryside	Ry Clerk	7-26-4	
John Taylor	Garryside lodger	Ry Clerk	7-26a-10	
William Mcintosh	Garryside lodger	Ry Engine Fireman	7-26b-11	
William Mclean	Garryside lodger	Ry Porter	7-28a-19	
Alexander Mcpherson	Garryside lodger	Ry Fireman	7-28b-20	

* A gravestone in Inverallan Cemetery, Grantown, reads: "John Calder engine driver Blair Atholl died Perth 14 December 1881 age 34, widow Margt. Cameron died 1882"

(Left) Will Stables at ease on a hurlie at the station entrance with a paper from the Menzies bookstall, seen behind.
(Atholl Country Life Museum)

Railway Employees : 1891 census

Name	Address	Job	Ref	1891?
Henry McLachlan	Blair Atholl son	Telegraph Clerk	7-1-4	
James Trotter	Blair Atholl visitor	Locomotive Stoker	7-6-19	
Alexander Joggie	Blair Atholl lodger	Railway Pointsman	7-11-1	
John Junor	Blair Atholl lodger	Railway Clerk	7-12-2	
Alexander Graham	Blair Atholl lodger	Railway Guard	7-16-13	
John Bonnyman	Blair Atholl lodger	Railway Pointsman	7-18-7	
Peter Stewart	Blair Atholl	Retired Railway Guard	7-20-15	Yes
William Dargavel	Blair Atholl	Railway Engine Driver	7-21-1	Yes
James Dargavel	Blair Atholl son	Railway Fireman	7-21-4	
James S Bruce	Blair Atholl lodger	Railway Fireman	7-25-19	
John Ross	Blair Atholl	Railway Pointsman	7-34-16	
Peter McNab	Blair Atholl lodger	Railway Engine Cleaner	7-35-4	
Charles Clunas	Blair Atholl lodger	Railway Stoker	7-36-5	
James Begbie	Blair Atholl lodger	Railway Engine Fireman	7-37-6	
John McGregor	Blair Atholl	Railway Surfaceman	7-38-7	Yes
John Matheson	Blair Atholl lodger	Engine Cleaner	7-38-9	
John A Rose	Blair Atholl lodger	Railway Engine Cleaner	7-39-13	
James McGillivray	Blair Atholl lodger	Railway Car Inspector	7-40-14	
Alexander Stewart	Blair Atholl	Gate Keeper	7-43-8	
Duncan McLennan	Blair Atholl	Station Master	7-53-3	
George McDonald	Blair Atholl	Railway Porter	7-54-6	
James Ross	Blair Atholl	Telegraph Lineman	7-55-10	
Murdoch McLean	Blair Atholl	Railway Engine Driver	7-56-15	
John Sinclair	Blair Atholl	Railway Car Inspector	7-57-2	
John McIntosh	Blair Atholl	Railway Pointsman	7-58-8	Yes
John McLachlan	Blair Atholl	Railway Engine Driver	7-59-14	Yes
Alexander Clark	Blair Atholl	Locomotive Foreman	7-60-19	

In Highland days, No. 6 Ben Armin *being turned. Note the snowplough stored on the spur.*
(Author's collection)

Railway Employees : 1901 census

Name	Address	Job	Ref	1891?
James Cameron	Cotts Garryside boarder	Engine Cleaner	7-2-11	
John Cameron	Cotts Garryside boarder	Engine Cleaner	7-2-12	
James Killar	Cotts Garryside boarder	Loco Fireman	7-5-7	
John Mcintosh	Cotts Garryside lodger	Ry Guard	7-10a-7	
John Mckenzie	Cotts Garryside boarder	Ry Pointsman	7-11-14	
Thomas W Clark	Cotts Garryside boarder	Ry Goods Clerk	7-11-15	
William Dargavel	Cotts Garryside	Clerk	7-14-23	Yes
James Seaton	Mill Cottage	Rly Relief Clerk	7-19a-9	
John Ross	Cott Ry Crossing	Ry Pointsman	7-22-14	Yes
Colin Munro	Cott Ry Crossing boarder	Ry Fireman	7-22-25	
Donald Mcgregor	Cott Ry Crossing son	Ry Surfaceman	7-23-2	
Alexander Mcgregor	Cott Ry Crossing son	Ry Stoker	7-23-3	
William Gault	Cott Ry Crossing boarder	Locomotive Fitter	7-23-5	
James Duff	Cott Ry Crossing boarder	Ry Carriage Inspector	7-23-6	
Kenneth Munro	Cott Ry Crossing	Ry Surfaceman	7-24-7	
William G Ross	Cott Ry Crossing servant	Ry Clerk	7-24a-13	
John Fraser	Cott Ry Crossing lodger	Ry Engine Driver	7-24a-14	
James Cameron	Cott Ry Crossing lodger	Ry Engine Cleaner	7-24a-16	
John Cameron	Cott Ry Crossing lodger	Ry Engine Fireman	7-24a-17	
John Young	Cott Ry Crossing	Ry Signal Fitter	7-25-18	
Joseph Adam	Cott Ry Crossing boarder	Ry Porter	7-25-22	
Alexander Mcintosh	Cott Ry Crossing boarder	Ry Pointsman	7-25-23	
Donald Fraser	Station House	Ry Stationmaster	7-34-15	
Peter Reid	Station Cottages	Ry Pointsman	7-37-21	
James Ross	Station Cottages	Telegraph Lineman	7-38-1	
James Dargavel	Station Cottages	Ry Engine Driver	7-39-9	Yes
Kenneth Gordon	Station Cottages	Ry Engine Driver	7-40-12	
John Mcintosh	Station Cottages	Ry Pointsman	7-41-17	Yes
Allan Tosh	Station Cottages	Loco Engine Driver	7-42-22	
William G Barclay	Station Cottages	Loco Engineer	7-43-1	
John Sinclair	Station Cottages	Ry Carriage Inspector	7-44-5	
James Bruce	Station Cottages	Ry Engine Driver	7-45-10	
John Mclachlan	Station Cottages	Ry Engine Driver	7-46-13	Yes
William Mcgregor	Back Lodge son-in-law	Loco Engine Fireman	7-47-21	

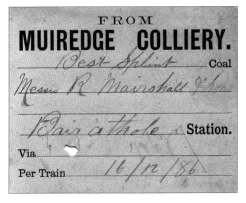

Railway Employees : 1911 census (Station Cottages only)

Name	Address	Job	Ref	1891?
John Ross Hugh Ross (son) Dan Tulloch (boarder) James Forbes (boarder) Robert Forbes (boarder)	Ry Cottages	Pointsman Post Office Learner * Engine Driver Pointsman Engine Cleaner	7-64-7	Yes Yes
Donald McGregor K McGregor (boarder) Angus McNaughton (boarder) George Gadsman (boarder)	Ry Cottages	Ry Surfaceman Fireman Foundry Worker * Foundry Worker *	7-65-16 7-65-20 7-65-21 7-65-22	Yes
Kenneth Munro John Munro (son) Kenneth Munro (son) Hugh Murray (boarder) A Gray (boarder) George Geddes (boarder)	Ry Cottages	Ry Surfaceman Post Man * Engine Cleaner Loco Fireman Loco Fireman Loco Fireman	7-66-23 7-66-25 7-66-26 7-66-27 7-66-28 7-66-29	Yes
William Cooke	Ry Cottages	Signal Fitter	7-67-30	
Donald Fraser	Station House	Station Master	7-68-1	Yes
James Ross	Station Cottages	Telegraph Lineman	7-69-9	Yes
John G Jameson William Jameson (son)	Station Cottages	Ry Porter Engine Cleaner	7-70-14 7-70-16	
John Ledingham Elizabeth Campbell (cousin) Theodore Ledingham (bro)	Station Cottages	Ry Engine driver Post Mistress * Engineer Draughtsman	7-71-23 7-71-27 7-71-28	
John Sinclair Hugh McLean (boarder)	Station Cottages	Ry Carriage Inspector Ry Surfaceman	7-72-29 7-72-33	Yes
John McLachlan	Ry Cottages	Ry engine driver	7-73-1	Yes
William G Barclay	Ry Cottages	Loco Superintendant	7-74-5	Yes
James Mannus	Ry Cottages	Ry engine driver	7-75-10	
* not an employee of the HR				

On same page, so not to leave out, also:				
William Cameron (boarder) Alexr McIntosh (boarder) Duncan McIntosh	Village of Blair	Porter Pointsman Engine Cleaner	7-63-1 7-63-3 7-63-6	Yes

Valuation Roll for 1898-1899 : all HR property in Blair Atholl

House at Blair Atholl Station	Henry Dunnet	£4-0-0
House at Blair Atholl Station	John Mackintosh	£4-0-0
House at Blair Atholl Station	Donald Macgregor	£4-0-0
House at Blair Atholl Station	Alex M'Leod	£4-0-0
House at Blair Atholl Station	John Sinclair	£4-0-0
House at Blair Atholl Station	Wm. G Barclay	£6-0-0
House at Blair Atholl Station	James Ross	£4-0-0
House at Blair Atholl Station	John M'Lachlan	£4-0-0
House at Blair Atholl Station	Kenneth Gordon	£4-0-0
House at Blair Atholl Station	Allan Tosh	£4-0-0
House at Blair Atholl Station	Hugh Shaw	£4-0-0
House at Blair Atholl Station	John Young	£4-0-0
House at Blair Atholl Station	vacant	£4-0-0
House & Garden, Blair Athole [sic]	Donald Fraser	£12-0-0
Gatekeeper's House & Garden	John Ross	£4-0-0

I've never established the location of the "Gatekeeper's House & Garden" listed every year in the valuation rolls with John Ross living there. Bearing in mind there were two crossings of the railway, the obvious one at the end of the platforms and the other one beside the saw mill lade, I wonder if the dormitory in fact became the gatekeeper's house before it became the bakehouse and garage.

The stalwart class of engine before Peter Drummond arrived on the scene in 1902, David Jones' Loch class pounded the metals for many years. In order to extend their useful life, over time these successful engines received replacement fireboxes, boilers and smokeboxes which greatly altered their appearance; the Caledonian design of boiler, for instance, sat some 9" higher than the Highland original. Allocated to Blair Atholl for local passenger and goods trains as well as occasional banking duties, this is No.14382 Loch Moy, ex-No.122, by now in its reboilered form, parked beside the two water tanks in the 1930s. These by then elderly Highland engines were eventually supplanted in the late 1930s by new LMS Stanier 2-6-2Ts, generally considered to be Stanier's least successful design. (Author's collection)

No.146 Skibo Castle in the all-green Highland Railway livery Peter Drummond introduced from September 1902. Built July 1902, so shiny all over that it must surely be freshly repainted. If the bowler-hatted gent is the gaffer, he will be William G Barclay. *(Author's collection)*

Blair Atholl Pictorial

General view of the main station building in 1963 still in original condition, with only the filigree decoration on the eaves now missing. (Howard Geddes)

The wing of the Duke's waiting room: all trains had to stop for the Duke of Atholl, and in 1963 it was still used occasionally even though it was apparent that the roof was sagging, the whole wing being demolished not very long afterwards. The pleasing symmetry was replaced by the lop-sided formation seen today; re-roofing with no overhang further destroyed the swiss-chalet style architectural integrity.
(Howard Geddes)

General view looking north, 19 March 1949. Notice the tiny angled station nameboards, simply fixed to the telegraph pole. Another can be seen beside the footbridge as well as on the opposite platform in the original photo - so different from the large display boards of earlier years. The coaches for the local passenger train are behind the platform, and there are hints of much activity, including shunting the daily local goods, with at least three plumes of steam rising on this sunny late winter morning.
(J L Stevenson, courtesy Hamish Stevenson)

General view looking south, No.14688 Thurso Castle *and No.14685* Dunvegan Castle *arrive hauling a Glasgow Buchanan St to Inverness train on 15 May 1928 in the morning on another sunny day. Note the large nameboard, notice also that a stretch of the northbound lay-by siding never had access from the platform.*
(Author's collection)

Jimmy McBean enjoying a browse, a gossip, and a smoke, when one could still justify a Station Bookstall – 1963. My Fair Lady now features on the billboard.
(Howard Geddes)

This waiting shed on the Down Line survives today and is reasonably well looked after. It replaced an older one that was built shortly after opening. Unusually for a wooden building it didn't burn down; instead the brick chimney collapsed which presumably was the reason for its replacement.
(Howard Geddes)

The Goods Shed. This had an office inside as well as a loading platform with a crane; road vehicles could draw up conveniently on the far side. But from a railway point of view, it was inconvenient being on a kickback siding that required some awkward shunting, maybe even with human muscle-power alone.
(Howard Geddes)

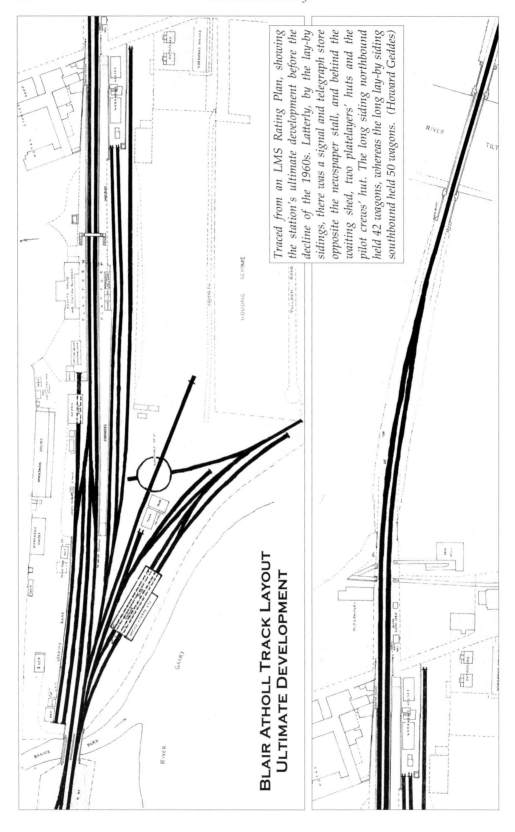

Traced from an LMS Rating Plan, showing the station's ultimate development before the decline of the 1960s. Latterly, by the lay-by sidings, there was a signal and telegraph store opposite the newspaper stall, and behind the waiting shed, two platelayers' huts and the pilot crews' hut. The long siding northbound held 42 wagons, whereas the long lay-by siding southbound held 50 wagons. (Howard Geddes)

**BLAIR ATHOLL TRACK LAYOUT
ULTIMATE DEVELOPMENT**

Minor buildings. Above left: James Marshall's Coal Office with, beyond, Steelyard gear limited to weighing 3 tons on the Weighbridge platform just visible. Above right: Every goods yard had its crane, this one now disused but in its day able to lift 5 tons. Right: A fascinating cluster of this-and-thats alongside the goods shed, the row of station cottages in background. (Howard Geddes)

We have seen very little of the southbound lay-by sidings. One was long enough to shunt a whole train out of the way allowing a following train to overtake. Ex-Caledonian Railway No.54467 simmers in the shorter Up Siding on 17 September 1954 waiting its turn to proceed all-stations to Perth at 1.30pm, taking only two coaches and leaving the rest behind. (Harold Bowtell/HRS Collection)

Four Struan Bankers said to stored out of use over the winter at the far end of the shed roads around 1930: Nos.15306, 15304, 15301, 15307 (ex Nos. 42, 43, 66, 44 respectively). The last two are in the first livery the LMS applied upon grouping in 1923. This colour scheme suited them exceedingly well: crimson red, fully lined, with the LMS coat of arms on the bunker and large numerals on the side tanks. The front two are in the second livery applied from 1928 on: black with red lining which can just be made out on the original photograph. No.15307 is the engine lamented in the poem on page 77. (HRS collection)

THE STRUAN BANKERS

This book is not about the Highland Railway as such, and it isn't appropriate to include general details of the company, its plant and its operations, and that includes its locomotives. However, there is one type of locomotive that is so tightly associated with Blair Atholl that an exception must be made. Some name the design as Class 39, mundanely after the first of the class which was so numbered, others call it the Banking Tank, while others entitle it the Struan Banker. As this latter name implies, these engines were designed specifically to assist trains up The Hill and those that were chosen for that task were, of course, shedded at Blair Atholl.

Introduced in the summer of 1909, these engines were the last design for the Highland Railway by the locomotive superintendent Peter Drummond before he moved to the Glasgow & South Western Railway. Until then the engines used at Blair Atholl for banking duties were never those in the first flush of youth. After the rather shaky start with locomotives unsuited to the terrain, as described in a previous chapter, through the exceptional designs of David Jones from 1870 on, the Highland Railway became to be often at the forefront of locomotive design, even though in the popular view less evident than the more glamorous and far bigger railway companies mostly radiating out of London. Nevertheless the HR had higher mountains to climb and just as long distances to travel, and as a consequence their locomotives were among the most powerful of their day. Trains rapidly got heavier around the turn of the century, in terms of both vehicle weight and numbers of vehicles hauled. The HR had its work cut out to provide locomotives powerful enough for the primary job of hauling trains; giving a bunk-up up The Hill was for more elderly locomotives.

No. 42 and No. 66 outside the engine shed, in the HR's final livery style which was introduced by Christopher Cumming after he took over as Locomotive Superintendent in 1915. The numberplates are new cast gunmetal; the original brass ones had been removed by Cumming's predecessor due to a brass famine at the beginning of the Great War. Note the standard HR shunting signal, unusual in being perched atop a high pole. The disc is turned away, which means "go", although there's no sign of movement of either men or machine. (HRS collection)

Because of the distances involved, all HR mainline locomotives had tenders, thus were the engines displaced from mainline revenue-earning duties and relegated to banking at Blair Atholl. Of no consequence going up The Hill, coming back down The Hill could be no joke, with the unsheltered crew facing whatever weather the mountains were deciding to throw at them. It's been described how the rain, the hail and the snow could be so fierce that they would blow sideways straight though the cab – in one side and out the other without touching the sides. Crews could rig a tarpaulin to cover the cab from roof to tender, but that only served to curtail visibility over the tender and still the freezing wind could swirl around the flapping edges making the crew's lives a misery.

With rail travel reaching its zenith in the Edwardian era, it was felt justified that locomotives be provided specially for banking between Blair Atholl and Dalnaspidal. At last, these replaced the draughty and elderly tender locomotives in use. They were designed for the job at hand. The result was a neat yet powerful engine that had small wheels to lay down that power, no high speed running being necessary. Instead of a tender carrying water, tanks that would usually be heavy with water provided even more adhesion, and there was also an integral coal bunker of sufficient capacity for the relatively short distances demanded. Best of all, there was a cosy cab that sheltered the crew whichever the direction of travel.

All four new Struan Bankers were allocated to Blair Atholl. Over the next couple of years

HR No. 43 in the post war period. Foreman Willie Bain is standing by the front buffer. Note the oil can sitting on the front steps – hope that doesn't get forgotten because it won't stay there for long! Note also the tablet catcher folded up on the cab side. The Highland had this apparatus throughout the system on single lines to allow drivers to proceed into the next section without having to stop and exchange tablets with the signalman by hand. The Struan Bankers were unique in that they had tablet catchers on both sides, thus allowing them to benefit from these arrangements whether running forwards or backwards. This would have come into use when running from Blair Atholl to Perth, not down The Hill from Dalnaspidal which by then was double-track. An oddity at Blair Atholl, but obvious when you think about it, is that there was a tablet-exchange apparatus on the lineside beside the level crossing, but it only 'gave-up' the tablet to the engine going south and entering the single line section but it had no means of receiving anything because on double-track no tablet was needed. The signalman told me that by the 1960s this apparatus was hardly ever used. (HRS collection)

another four were delivered. Blair Atholl never needed any more than four, so the extra engines were used elsewhere on the system on various services. Somewhat ironically, their small wheels meant they couldn't keep up on the flat bits leading to the stiff haul up to Slochd, whereas The Hill was an unrelenting climb all the way from Blair Atholl – you only have to drive along the road towards Bruar to see the railway urging upwards on an ever increasing embankment.

The timetable over the Highland main line, especially northbound, was such that there were bursts of activity at certain times of the day, followed by periods of quiet, so much of the time was sitting around waiting. The main goods trains came through Blair Atholl in the middle of the night. This meant that one or two banking engines were generally speaking ready on hand twenty-four hours a day. Then in summer especially, one timetabled train would often run in two portions, and at the busiest times anything up to five portions could be sent out from Perth, one after the other. The number of portions and their loading tended to be relatively unpredictable, with not enough time to get an engine prepared from cold if there was a sudden influx at Perth, so this unpredictability also had to be covered at Blair Atholl. All this meant that the Struan Bankers were under-used, although they did get used for the daily local goods and for the local passenger trains to Perth. Nevertheless Struan Bankers had to be in steam, coaled, watered and ready for action. People still remember two or three Banking Tanks lined up just outside the loco shed, almost like a husky team waiting to be unleashed. Also recalled is the practice of one sitting opposite the south Signal Cabin on the Up line, waiting for the Down train's arrival, whereupon a smartish trip up to Tilt Viaduct and back onto the train would take less time than any necessary duties on the station platform. Reminiscent of 1863 when there were complaints about engines standing around the old wooden engine shed

The fireman has stoked up No.15306 to the very gills on 27 September 1935, the fire making plenty of smoke. With the safety valves blowing off showing there is already a full head of steam, the crew are about to move out of the yard and back onto the northbound train waiting in the platform. No.15306 is on the road leading from the turntable and water tanks; the gradient of the coal wagon road as it rises to a less inconvenient shovelling-height can be discerned. The train engine appears to be No.14690 Dalcross Castle. *(HRS collection)*

spoiling the neighbours' washing, much the same was happening seventy or so years later - one wonders to what level of complaint.

The rules of engagement were often honoured in the breach, but generally Bankers banked from the back of goods trains and piloted from the front of passenger trains. Trains already double-headed would be banked from the rear – and yes, two at the front and one behind did happen, although I'm not aware of any photographs of what must have been quite a sight and sound. In Highland days the Bankers were supposed always to be coupled to the train, whereas in LMS days Bankers could push goods trains without being coupled.

If all went well, the train and banker drivers would exchange whistles that each was ready, and off the train would go, each loco sharing the load up to Dalnaspidal. Inevitably, it didn't always happen like that. Instances have been noted when the train would leave Blair Atholl leaving the Banker behind. The Banker would then take off in pursuit, hopefully catching up and making contact with the train without too much drama to crews, train or passengers. A Banker would even occasionally get left behind on The Hill itself, again a bit of dextrous driving would be required of the Banker's crew to retrieve the situation, usually with not a lot of help from the main engine crew who were either unaware or unappreciative of their temporary separation.

Two water columns were provided at the end of the northbound platform, spaced a Castle apart (the class of engine that was the HR's mainstay express engine from 1900), so that both engines of a double-headed train could take on water at the same time. Pretty well all trains stopped at Blair Atholl and took water at one of the two water columns. Coupling the Banker to the front of a single-headed passenger train at Blair Atholl would be easily done in the time

Three Struan Bankers hanging around, fully coaled. 15306 left, 15307 middle, 15304 right. Note the extra coupling at the back of 15304. This isn't something I've seen before and I wonder if this was a belt-and-braces standard precaution when piloting a heavy train and perhaps working rather too much harder than the train engine. The Banking Tank in front has a different style of coupling, one normally associated with goods trains. For once, at least one set of engine shed doors are closed, hinting that this may be Sunday when things were much quieter. *(HRS collection)*

available. The Banker would simply roll out from its waiting place in front of the engine shed and back up. To achieve this under proper control, there were two standard HR disk shunt signals, this time a Banker apart, on high poles outside on one of the shed roads. Thus, two Bankers at a time could be waiting each to be released singly onto the main line under the signalman's control, whilst a third could be hanging around on the loop past the shed.

This arrangement would also apply to goods trains. If the Banker was not in the waiting position down at the South Cabin (maybe a southbound train was blocking the way, or for any other reason one can concoct), then the goods train would have to draw forward clear of the engine yard exit to allow the Banker to move onto the rear. Drawing forward a heavy, loose-coupled goods train is not a simple task, and if not executed with care, apart from the danger of physically breaking couplings, the snatch upon starting transmitted through forty or fifty couplings could easily throw the poor guard to the floor, only to be followed by the compression caused in the stopping which would repeat the humiliation if he had meantime managed to clamber upright. The chances of bad humour and a shouting match would be quite high, especially as the rules at one time required there to be two brake vans meaning there were two guards to be inconvenienced. I have no evidence, but I wouldn't be at all surprised that the main train started off and simply carried on, leaving the Banker to escape the confines of the loco yard and catch up as catch can.

Bankers came off at Dalnaspidal, sometimes Dalwhinnie. At busy times, they would gather and all come down The Hill coupled together as one train. At other times, they would hitch a lift on a passing southbound train – this saved time and a train path. Another variation was that a Banker coming down The Hill could wait at Struan for a northbound train, rather than returning to base.

The Blair Atholl men did a sterling job over many years, at times monotonous whilst at other times demanding in terms of both driving skills and hardiness in the face of appalling weather. One such was John Macpherson who retired from LMS service on 31 March 1925, the subject of this plaintive poem by John Macdonald, the stationmaster at Dalguise. Macpherson's 'true and trusty steed' was the Struan Banker No. 44. The driver may well have been "Brandy Jock" who is in the photograph in the chapter Men And Machine of the shed men of Blair Atholl.

Driver John MacPherson's Farewell to His Engine

I paced the track in times gone by
With Barney, Loch and Ben,
And climbed Drumochter's barren crest
With Castle and with Glen;
I parted with them all, without
A sight or heartache sore
Such as I feel in saying goodbye,
To thee, sweet 44.

John Macdonald - Poems of a Roadside Station Master - 1925

The water tank at Blair Athole. This is one of only two reasonable views of the water tank I know of. The access ladder to the tank itself can be seen clearly. This and a couple of other photos are not clear enough to determine whether the tank is open to the sky or enclosed; but there are signs of perhaps a venting chimney or even the feed pipe itself, as well as a crawl-board across the top of the tank and presumably a feed control mechanism beside the top of the ladder. This is pure supposition on my part, but that venting-chimney could be a chimney through from the base - with a fire lit down below in a simple brazier known as a fire-devil, this would provide a crude but reasonably effective measure against the water in the tank freezing. The main lade can be seen above the tank, coming past the corn mill, whilst the loop through the cluttered saw mill can be seen as it rejoins.
(Author's collection, part of GWW B0487, which is an enlargement print from B487)

This is the only other good view; unfortunately this extract is not the best quality but is included for its rarity. Three sets of buffer stops at the ends of the two lay-by sidings and the old engine shed siding can just be made out - this is where the cottages would be built. The level crossing is between those and the little pointsman's hut.
(part of GWW F0184)

Blair Atholl's Water Supply

For nigh on a century, more than 230 households, businesses and schools in Blair Atholl and Bridge of Tilt had their drinking water supplied by the Highland Railway and its successors right up to Network Rail. For free! For ever! But recently this unique arrangement has passed into history, for Network Rail paid Scottish Water to connect the village to the mains which, as fate and fortune had it, already passed right through the village, with nary a branch left or right, on its way to Calvine and Struan from a reservoir high above Killiecrankie beyond Old Faskally Farm. Needless to say, the water would no longer be free, but at least it would be clear and pure, where before (just run a bath at the Atholl Arms...) it was varying shades of brown and sometimes articles of uncertain provenance would appear - mostly dead but sometimes a bit wriggly.

This chapter describes how water was supplied by and to the railway, and hence to the village. I have no doubt there are other sources of information which I haven't unearthed, but I have relied on what is available from the local Lude and Atholl Estates over which the supply ran.

It has long been believed locally that the Railway was required by Act of Parliament to supply free water for ever. I'll show that in actual fact a binding agreement was made only in 1926, formalising what appears to have been only an informal agreement between the various parties previously. Indeed, Scottish Water called the arrangement "a historical quirk" and Network Rail called it "an outdated anomaly", both saying in 2006 that the supply had existed for 95 years, i.e. since 1911. When the railway no longer required a water supply for operational purposes, maintaining that water supply was simply an unjustifiable overhead, even if the commitment remained and even if railway property such as the station building still required a water supply, Network Rail and its predecessors did not properly maintain the water supply in some very basic ways with the resultant dirty water causing many complaints. It is hardly surprising that previous efforts to offload their commitment onto the conventional water supplier failed. But finally, it was inevitable that this pleasingly quirky but expensive anomaly passed into history.

Blair Atholl's Mills and Mill Lades

There were many mill lades supplying the mills in and around Blair Atholl, some coming off the several burns and others being sourced from springs. We are concerned with two, the most significant of the bunch. Their approximate routes are shown in the map overleaf.

The first, which we shall name Blair Lade for convenience, is also the oldest. John Kerr's Water Mills Of Atholl states that there was a mill (and hence mill lade) shown there in 1600 but it is known to have existed long before then. Known as "Katherine's Mill", its successor, built in the 1830s, is the preserved mill open and working today. The mill lade comes off River Tilt via some quite substantial buttresses and sluice gates, and eventually runs into River Garry. Blair Lade actually split into two, the branch-lade serving an almost equally old waulk mill which was itself succeeded by a lint mill in 1783, and which in turn became the saw mill which closed in the 1940s but whose buildings remained until the 1960s. The main Lade is still very much in existence, its run obvious and in use, by the mill as well as by a large posse of quacky ducks; and if you know where to look, the other lade can also be spotted, even though much of it ran underground until it rejoins the main Lade just beyond the Corn Mill. Both ran under the railway, and both culverts are still there.

Routes of lades and pipes superimposed upon 1st Edition OS 6" map of 1867. The old mill lades are shown dotted - Lude Lade is at the top and Blair Lade below. The approximate route of the railway supply pipeline is shown as a solid line - it ends at the Water Tank.

In the Track Plan on page 16, the temporary wooden engine shed can be seen, opposite the Blair Athole Hotel; Blair Lade is running through top to bottom between the Corn Mill and the Saw Mill, and the lade branch through the Saw Mill can be made out, partly underground. The Water Tank is also marked, just beside where the lade runs under the railway, on the down side. With no sign on any map of the railway's pipe rising to the surface, an oddity of the whole set up is that it had to cross the mill lade - unless it was rather near the surface of the railway solum, it would have passed underneath one or even both the lades. With the new water supply in place, these old pipes will still be there. One hopes future developments don't dig them up by mistake - who knows what is holding back the entire the Fender Burn from diverting down this pipeline.

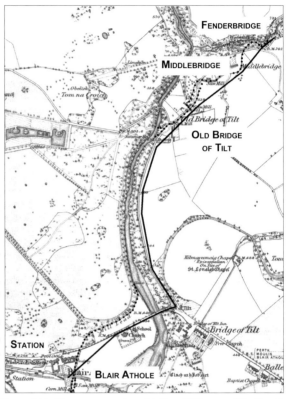

(drawing Howard Geddes, map courtesy National Library of Scotland)

The second, which we shall name Lude Lade because it is on the Lude Estate, served three mills at Old Bridge Of Tilt: two saw mills and a corn mill. Records going back to before 1700 show that the upstream saw mill used to be a waulk mill and the downstream mill a lint mill. A map of 1815 shows the corn mill, named Mill Tomkindrochet, and the lade. All three mills were supplied by this one lade coming off Fender Burn above Fenderbridge (known today as "Postie's Bridge") which flowed back into River Tilt a little further downstream. Mill of Kindrochet was described as an excellent meal mill in 1840, and all three were in operation when the railway was built in 1863.

Water Supply – Stage 1

As already noted, when the railway opened in 1863, a stone-base water tank was erected beside the main running line, right beside the main Blair Lade. As far as I can tell, the railway's water supply has always entered railway property at the juncture of the old water tank and Blair Lade. From its position, it must have been the intention at least that the water tank be fed from the lade. This would require some physical mechanism to extract the water and raise it into the tank itself. I am not aware of any such pumping arrangement. It's hard to imagine pumping by hand, so perhaps the water was indeed supplied right from the start in pipes from higher up Glen Fender, thus providing the necessary head of pressure to fill the tank without any manual or mechanically-assisted pumping. The standard mechanism in filling a storage tank is the familiar ball-cock which supplies water to a certain level then automatically cuts off. But I get the impression that the tank at Blair Athole was fed through a simple on-off valve, manually controlled. In either case, access to the mechanism would be required, and indeed an access ladder can be seen in the photos of the water tank.

Original I&PJR drawings survive but they do not show how the tank was supplied, so it's not possible to conclude what the original arrangements were. They also do not show any facilities to supply engines directly from the tank, but I can infer from the design of the stone base itself that there were no facilities; instead, water was piped along to water columns (in effect simple stand pipes) at the end of each platform from where locomotives could be replenished. There is no sign of a water column by the loco shed – another indication that the shed was temporary.

When the temporary engine shed was replaced by the 'new' stone shed some distance west towards the Banvie Burn, a new water tank was provided there too. Whatever method was used at the original site, the new site isn't adjacent to a water flow. From the future history of Blair Atholl's water supply, there can be little doubt that the water still came from the same source, and not from Banvie Burn. To support this further, the OS map surveyed in 1898 does not show any pump-house alongside the Banvie Burn such was there many years later. There is also no mention and no evidence of any mechanical assistance with the new water tank, so I have little doubt that even by now the water was extracted high up in nearby Glen Fender and gravity let to do the work – there would be an ample head of water to fill the tank through sheer pressure. A 1910 map confirms that water was taken from Lude Lade quite close to Fender Burn, and well before the Saw Mill, into a tank, and then piped down to the railway. A later plan shows the pipe entering railway property at the site of the old water tank.

Whatever the means of extraction, the I&PJR would have had to have come to some agreement with the local estate owners (Atholl and Lude in this case) for permission, as well as agreeing practical arrangements with the local mill owners who were sharing the water flows. If extracting from the mill lades, the I&PJR was in no position to argue if Lude decided to deprive the railway of water by closing his sluice on his Lade serving the Mills on his Estate. On the other hand, if extracting from Glen Fender, the I&PJR could well deprive the working mills downstream of their own source of power. There clearly was a high degree of co-operation, although I haven't seen any actual agreements from these early days. So far also, I haven't seen any evidence that there was a Statutory Responsibility, enforceable by Act Of Parliament, to supply free water in perpetuity to the village; on the contrary, there is evidence to suggest there was nothing of the sort.

Water Supply – Stage 2

The plan of 1910 mentioned above has survived - just; it is the Highland Railway's only plan so far found and is in very poor condition. It shows that there was a pre-existing tank, possibly a simple settling tank rather than for storage, right beside Fender Burn at Middlebridge Cottages, so presumably the intake was through a simple sluice gate. The outflow was piped across the fields on the other side of the Lade (so the outlet must have gone underneath the Lade) to the junction of the public roads leading down from Tirinie and Monzie. All this was on Lude land. The pipe evidently followed the public road down to the old A9 and across the Bridge Of Tilt, where it then went diagonally across fields (belonging to the Atholl Estate) to the railway; it went underneath the railway and paralleled it until reaching the site of the old water tank. It looks as though it travelled alongside the railway tracks and hence went over both branches of Blair Lade, as well as under two level crossings. I can imagine this would give a very satisfactory head of water supplying the station's water tanks without the need for any pumping; I can also imagine that any filtration was crude. And I expect the supply was

The Intake Dam. It's almost impossible to get a decent view of the dam itself; this view required hacking through a jungle of wild untended growth on the side of a slippery slope to a thorough soaking. The intake sluice is just about visible.

(Howard Geddes)

controlled with not a lot more than the operation of outlet valves on the Glen Fender tank, and sluice gates off the Fender Burn. I wonder how long one watertankful down at the station would last? Perhaps it required a refill only once a week or so, and therefore there would be no need for continuous supply? That seems most likely, given that the Mills themselves would need continuous supplies.

It is probable that this Stage 2 was built in 1891, because there is a reference in a 1926 agreement (see below) to such a storage tank by Middlebridge, and I shouldn't think any significant development had happened in between. I believe that this 1891 storage tank was superseded by the 1910 improvement, although I'm not clear why it should have then been referred to in 1926.

Basing all this on a single plan means that I cannot tell whether non-railway locations in the village were supplied at this time with water or not. Also, the situation between 1863 and 1891 is unclear - in other words, it's uncertain when the pipeline was first built.

The Intake Ball. This is not a damaged photo: half obscured by water reflection, this is looking directly down upon the actual intake. A rusty perforated metal sphere no bigger than a football on the bed of Fenderburn. This was the cause of the whole situation – this intake ball used to be three feet or so above the bed but over the years the bed has silted right up almost submerging the intake pipe completely. Network Rail had long declined to dredge the burn by the dam, so inevitably bits and pieces roll along the burn bed, through what holes remain unburied, and into the water supply. It doesn't take much to imagine the inevitable consequences - fortunately mostly discoloured water, but we won't mention the dead sheep that had to be hauled out some way up Fenderburn a few years ago. *(Howard Geddes)*

Water Supply – Stage 3

We are fortunate that the plan is not the only surviving record from the 1910/11 improvement. Highland Council has a Project Estimates Book in its archives which provides quite copious details of the works involved.

The 1910 map (which is not in said book) shows the new arrangements. A new Intake Dam someway upstream opposite the settlement of Fenderbridge was to be built, with a new 6" pipe paralleling the Fender Burn under Postie's Bridge into a new Filter beside the public road and then connecting to the existing pipe with a new 5" pipe beside the mill lade. Regrettably the plan is only partial but I don't think anything significant is missing.

The initial proposal of 25 July 1910, with detailed costing totalling £401, comprised a concrete dam, a timber scouring sluice in the dam, a roofed filter with a gathering drain, and a 5" cast-iron pipe between sluice and filter, a distance of 190 yards. Revised details of 24 August 1910 result in an increase to £529: the filter capacity is rated at 4000 gallons per hour at 700 gallons per square yard, the filter being 50' by 25', filled 3' deep with 140 cubic yards of 'filtering material' (which cost £49). 5" piping is specified throughout (although in the event 6" pipes were used between dam and filter), and there's extra work now identified for a culvert and at a public road (I presume the adjacent road by Middlebridge), plus 'suitable connections' at the water tank (which might refer to an existing underground storage behind Middlebridge rather than the water tanks down at the station). In a manner similar to railways taking over canals, it seems that the new supply used Lude Lade itself, with 15" fire-clay pipes being laid on the bed of the lade 'forming suitable dams'. I interpret this to mean that Lude Lade's intake off Fender Burn was abandoned, with the new intake being the railway's own further upstream, which in turn used the now superseded lade channel for some 30yds downstream of the filter, before splitting into the existing Lude Lade and the new railway supply pipeline by means of an undefined nature. There was also a 'sand washer' in addition to the main filter; I don't know what it was but it was cheap with a 'surface box' costing a mere 10/-.

Two alternative estimates show a scheme using two Bell's Patent Mechanical Filters, one a pair of 4ft diameter the other a pair of 6ft diameter, totalling £544 and £911 respectively. There's a sketch of the timber shed required for the smaller plant, at 16ft x 11ft much smaller than 50ft x 25ft, which might explain why it was looked into. However, the higher prices and what appears to be a lesser capacity meant that these alternatives were rejected.

There follows thoroughly detailed calculations of materials required. A contract was awarded to Messrs Ramage & Cooper of Perth and work quickly got under way because an interim payment of £110/-/- was made for work completed up to 13 November 1910; a detailed measurement by the HR of their work shows an achievement worth £106/11/-. Final measurement by the HR took place on 13 December 1910, Ramage's final contribution to the project being worth £300/19/8 of which £30/19/8 was held back until the Highland Railway took over ongoing responsibility for the maintenance of the plant after six months.

The distance from dam to filter was 190 yards; from filter to 'point A' on the plan 540 yards. This appears to be the extent of Ramage & Cooper's contract, 'point A' being outside the Waulk Mill at Old Bridge of Tilt. There is a hint that the Highland Railway supplied at least some, perhaps the majority, of the materials, which might explain why Ramage's work was so much less than the £529 overall estimate. That they only worked down to 'point A' suggests that the rest of the pipe-work from there to the loco yard remained the same. Notice how quickly the works were completed - if only today....

I'm not entirely sure when the second water tank at Blair Atholl was erected, but during these works, two estimates were produced. The first specified the direct connection between the two tanks by means of a 12" pipe underneath each tank - total cost £6/-/-! The second was for 'connection [of the tanks] to mains' - I really cannot make out for sure what's going on but perhaps existing pipery was being extended and improved around and about the tanks; was this because the second tank was being built at the same time? One point of note is that the 'new' 12" pipes weren't new - they and 'an old 12" valve' came from Moy, where they were lifted (dug up?!) and transported to Blair Atholl for reuse.

Water Supply – Stage 4

I do not know when villagers started being connected to the railway's own supply, but the pre-existing arrangements were formalised between the Duke of Atholl and the LMS in an agreement of 20 October 1926. This tells us that: "the Railway Company have water led to their Railway Station at Blair Atholl from the Fender Burn by means of: a six-inch pipe from the Intake Dam in Fender Burn to a Reservoir and Filter constructed by them in [1910] on subjects acquired by them from the proprietors of the Estate of Lude; a five-inch pipe from the said Reservoir and Filter to a Tank constructed by them in [1891] on the said Estate of Lude; a four-inch pipe from the said Tank to said Railway Station at Blair Atholl." And there were already four connections to: the

The Filter and Settling Shed. Close to the public road, the main shed nestles away almost unnoticed. A small shed behind was the 'purification plant' where the chlorine was stored and dispensed. The exposed pipe from the intake dam passed through and various pipes allowed the chlorine to be mixed with the water, using a pump to drip feed the requisite amount throughout the day. Chlorine levels were checked daily, the amount added being altered manually. The Lude gamekeeper was responsible for this, keeping a daily log of events and the water/chlorine concentrations. I don't understand the readings, but a page for September 2006 shows one pump blockage and two heavy rains, and chlorine concentrations varied from 0.05 to 2.2 mg/l. The treated water fountained up in the settling shed to settle through the filter bed, and away it went to the villagers' taps. And that's all there was to it. (Howard Geddes)

Schoolhouse, the Parish Church, the houses at Garryside and Blair Castle Back Lodge, with the Estate now (1926) wanting more.

The first key statement is: "there is no formal agreement between the parties hereto regarding the water led from the Fender Burn to the said Railway Station as aforesaid and it is expedient that the arrangement between the parties should be reduced to writing", so that fatally undermines the idea of any long-standing Statutory Commitment.

The second is: "The [Duke] agrees to the Railway Company continuing to take in perpetuity free of charge a supply of water as they at present do from the said Fender Burn ....". Contrary to the previously generally-held understanding, this in itself does not compel the railway to supply the village. However, what did commit the railway was the agreement that the Duke was entitled, free of charge, to lay his own pipes and draw water off the railway's pipes for his and his tenants' own use: in order to comply with this, the railway of course had to maintain their pipes in working order for as long as the Duke insisted on his entitlement. Not only that, the implication was that the water had to be potable, hence the need for chlorination at the railway's expense.

The Duke could extend his pipery in any way he desired "subject to the approval of the Railway Company's Engineer, which approval shall not be unreasonably withheld".

An intriguing clause states that: "In the event of justifiable complaint of lack of pressure ... the Railway Company shall on request of the [Duke] but only during the period from First June to Thirtieth September in any year provide and maintain a Ball valve at the end of the said four-inch pipe leading into the tank at the Engine Shed at Blair Atholl Station. The Railway Company if required by the [Duke] shall put said ball valve in operation for such period during every Sunday as may be deemed necessary by the [Duke]...". I think this means that the Duke could insist that the railway not fill their water tanks on Summer Sundays.

There was literally one working drawing of the system showing the pipe lines - its condition was unbelievably poor but it was all that anyone had to show where the pipes were - there was not even a spare copy. Little wonder that the days of free supply of water to the village were numbered. It shows that a pipe came down the public road from Monzie, over the road Bridge of Tilt, along the ex-A9 past the Parish Church and Schoolhouse, and then cut across a field to the railway, which it crossed. The route is clear enough but it looks as though there were two pipes in parallel. Possibly the Saw Mill and Corn Mill were connected. A branch off the pipe carried on down the public road by the level crossing to the cottage beside the Mill but no further. The main pipe continued alongside the railway

The Purification Plant – interior. Alistair Stephen, normally the Lude Estate gamekeeper but also retained by Network Rail, taking a daily reading on their behalf. The main pipe is literally underfoot, completely exposed. (Howard Geddes)

and railway cottages, cut to the back of the down platform and went between the sidings, with a branch off to the Station Building and Boiler House on the up platform. Another branch cut back across the railway to service the outside toilets by the goods shed, as well as all the cottages in the goods yard (Goat Lane) and Back Lodge across the road. The main pipe finally angled across and split into two to feed the two water tanks. I infer that there was separate pipework feeding water from the water tanks to the water columns as well as the toilets by the water tanks and any taps etc in the loco shed.

There may have been a similar agreement with the Lude Estate, but only an undated LMS plan has surfaced, showing yet another replacement pipe coming down Glen Fender, which connections off to various dwellings. There is however a more modern plan showing the pipery in Bridge Of Tilt – that part of Blair Atholl village on the other side of the road bridge and presumably part of the Lude Estate. Network Rail's problems were clearly exacerbated by not only the Lude Estate's pipes now connecting most of the village there, but also by the County Council taking supply off Lude's pipes to supply all the new housing down Invertilt and St Adamson Roads.

The final development on the pipeline was the building of a simple brick hut in the middle of a field behind Middlebridge over the underground pipe. Abandoned now, and with an inspection access some 50 yards away still poking out of the middle of the field, its precise use was never satisfactorily explained, but it was proudly proclaimed to be named Elizabeth's Shed because it was built (by BR) at the time of the Coronation. Another railway structure in the oddest of places.

The Final Curtain

A rather more recent development is Lude Estate's own hydroelectric scheme which takes its water immediately downstream of the intake dam, using its own intake facilities. This supplies most of Lude estate today, so there was great consternation when Network Rail announced that they would simply demolish their intake dam when Scottish Water took over the village supply. This would have been little short of catastrophic, because the hydroelectric intake was designed such that it depended upon the intake dam to act as a barrier. My understanding is that the issue was resolved by Lude buying the intake dam (thereby relieving Network Rail of its liability if the intake dam fails or someone falls in).

With Scottish Water taking over the water supply, all the existing pipelines and works became redundant. Plans of the whereabouts of much of the existing equipment were hopelessly inadequate, so most of the railway's pipe-work has been abandoned, to remain buried and lost. And so, the end came to an intriguing example of mutually-beneficial symbiosis between the railway and the community it served.

However, the most important structure, the Highland Railway's own Dam built in 1910, will remain in continuous daily use for the foreseeable future. The supply of water from the surrounding countryside to the railway station seems to have escaped the attention of both railway enthusiasts and local historians, presumably because much of the infrastructure is not only outside the railway fence but also under the ground, hidden and away from all ken. Yet not only did minor burns have their water extracted, but whole lochs were formed by containment embankments to provide a reliable source year round. Blair Atholl's arrangement was extremely rare in that the waters were used for sustain humans as well as engines, but at the same time entirely typical of an arrangement which was repeated time and again at nearly every station on the Highland Railway.

Queen Victoria's Visit - 1863

Queen Victoria visited Blair Athole station on 15 September 1863, just a few days after its opening. It tickled me immensely that the monarch of the day had surveyed not the slightly grand edifice of later years but a little wooden shed.

Down the years, a myth has been perpetuated that Queen Victoria was not at all enamoured by the prospect of railways, whether travelling on them or noting their impact on the countryside, especially in her beloved Highlands. There is some pretty direct evidence for this, for instance:

Wednesday, October 3, 1866
We now entered Strath Tay... The Tay is a fine large river... Now an unsightly and noisy railroad runs along this beautiful glen, from Dunkeld as far as Aberfeldy.
(Diary of Queen Victoria, describing an excursion from Dunkeld to Tummel side, Glen Lyon and Taymouth Castle)

However, the Queen did travel by rail, especially to and from Balmoral. Of course various vehicles were purpose-built or put at her sole disposal over the years, and it has been authoritatively stated that train journeys always excited her. Nonetheless, the Queen stipulated that the speed of her special train should be limited to 35mph by day and 25mph by night.

It is well-documented that Queen Victoria and Prince Albert fell in love with the Scottish Highlands upon their visit in 1842 (the first state visit since 1651), to the extent that they bought the Balmoral Estate in 1852 and by 1855 had built the present Castle. Although there were several, almost annual, visits to Scotland, the very first mention of the Highland Railway was in 1861:

Wednesday, October 9, 1861
We passed by the Bruar, and the road to the Falls of the Bruar, but could not stop. The Duke [of Athole] took us through a new approach, which is extremely pretty; but near which, I cannot help regretting, the railroad will come, as well as along the road by which we drove through the Pass of Drumouchter [sic].
(Diary of Queen Victoria, describing a journey from the inn at Dalwhinnie to Blair Castle)

To put this into perspective, the first sod of the Inverness & Perth Junction Railway from Forres to Dunkeld was cut on 17 October 1861 at Forres, so there must have been at least some signs of the impending works as the Queen travelled, even if only surveyors' markers.

Around the time of the railway's opening, Queen Victoria had learned that the Duke was terminally ill, no doubt by way of the Duchess who was a Lady in Waiting and a favoured companion. The Queen had a demonstrably close friendship with the family, having visited Blair Castle on several previous occasions, notably in 1844. She was thus concerned enough that she decided to break her planned train journey from Windsor to Balmoral at Perth, and pay a visit.

Friday, September 11, 1863
Nobody is to know it, but while the Royal Children rest, H M would run up in a Special Train to Blair & back again ... H M would change Her dress & come on directly & return after ½ an hour's time or so by the special to Perth.
(Letter from Lady Augusta Bruce, formerly Lady in Waiting to the Queen's late mother, to Duchess Anne)

Note this is but two days after the opening of the line. So, on September 15, only six days after opening, the first royal journey over Highland metals took place. Queen Victoria was accompanied by Lady Augusta Bruce, Princess Helena Victoria ('Lenchen', the Queen's third daughter born 1846) and General Sir Charles Grey (private secretary to the Queen) who had arranged all things security-wise and otherwise. It would appear that the Royal Train remained at Perth, the Special Train consisting of just a single saloon carriage for the royal party and another carriage for railway personnel. According to newspaper reports, the train departed at 9.30am. As already noted, although the I&AJR worked the I&PJR line, they were using other companies' engines, so the special train could have been hauled by a Scottish Central Railway or even a Caledonian Railway locomotive.

Balmoral, Tuesday, September 15, 1863

At twenty minutes to eight we reached Perth, where we breakfasted and dressed, and at twenty minutes past nine I left with Lenchen, Augusta Bruce and General Grey for Blair, going past Dunkeld, where we had not been since 1844, and which is so beautifully situated, and Pitlochry, through the splendid Pass of Killiecrankie (which we so often drove through in 1844) past Mr Butter's place at Faskally, on to Blair, having a distant peep at the entrance to Glen Tilt, and Schiehallion, which it made and makes me sick [with longing] to think of. At the small station were a few people - the poor Duke's Highlanders (keepers), the dear Duchess, Lord Tullibardine, and Captain Drummond of Megginch.

The Duchess was much affected...

We drove at once to the house .... (Diary of Queen Victoria)

Note that Killiecrankie Station had not been built, so the Pass presumably still appeared relatively unsullied from the train. The train arrived at Blair Athole 'punctual to the minute' at 10.35am, the Queen's coach stopping opposite a length of cloth in the Murray tartan which stretched across the platform to a waiting carriage, where Duchess Anne was ready to greet the Queen. A guard of honour of Athole Highlanders was on parade on the platform, commanded by the Duchess' son, Lord Tullibardine, heir to the 6th Duke, and Captain John Drummond. The Queen alighted and went to the Duchess immediately: their "interview was of the most melancholy description, Her Majesty and the Duchess embracing each other tenderly, and both burst into tears, while the onlookers were deeply affected". Because of the sadness of the occasion, there was no cheering from the crowd of about 200 people who had gathered outside the station, as the royal party set off for the castle, escorted by the Highlanders.

The Queen stayed for an hour at the castle, and there was much surprise that the Duke was able to escort her back to the station, as he was then so ill. Arriving at the station at 11.40am, the Queen spoke to The Hon. T. C. Bruce, the brother of the Governor of India as well as the chairman of the I&PJR, and expressed her satisfaction with the new line and the pleasure it gave her to pass through such magnificent scenery.

Balmoral, Tuesday, September 15, 1863

The poor Duke insisted on going with me to the station, and he went in the carriage with the Duchess and me. At the station he got out, walked about, and gave directions. I embraced the dear Duchess and gave the Duke my hand, saying, 'Dear duke, God bless you!' He had asked permission that his men, the same who had gone through the glen on that happy day two years ago, might give me a cheer, and he led them on himself. Oh! it was so dreadfully sad! To think of the contrast to the time two years ago, when my darling was so well and I so happy with him, and just beginning to recover from my great sorrow for dearest Mama's death – looking forward

...... Oh! how little we know what is before us! How uncertain is life! I felt very sad, but was so much occupied with the poor Duke for whom I truly grieved that I did not feel the trial of returning to Blair in such terribly altered circumstances, as I should otherwise have done.

(Diary of Queen Victoria)

Having made her final farewell to the Duke, the Queen's special train returned to Stanley Junction, the Royal Train having travelled onwards from Perth to Stanley. The royal party resumed their journey north to Aberdeen and Balmoral at 12.45pm.

Bruce travelled with the engine driver in the cab for the journeys from Perth and back to Stanley Junction. While, in case of breakdown, Andrew Dougall, the general manager of both the I&AJR and I&PJR, travelled in the train along with several engineers and Thomas Fyfe, the secretary of the P&DR. Although Joseph Mitchell was the Engineer, I conclude that he was not present, since he himself does not refer to this event.

Balmoral, Tuesday, September 15, 1863

At Stanley Junction we joined the others, and proceeded as usual to Aboyne, whence we drove in open carriages ... and reached Balmoral at twenty minutes past six. It was very cold..

(Diary of Queen Victoria)

The visit was memorialised by the following verse.

The Queen's Visit To The Duke Of Athole
15th September 1863

Let Athole's hills the story tell;
and every Highland Stream,
In ever-flowing numbers, swell
The music of the theme:-
The beauty, and the lovingness,
The kindness of the scene;
The goodness and the charity,
Of Britain's gracious Queen!
For never has a woman's love
More touchingly been seen;
And never yet has pity shone
With brighter, holier beam,

Than when, by Tay's fair flowing tide,
The Monarch turned her steps aside,
Regardless of the toil to come
ere yet she reach her Highland home:
Thoughtless of all, except the deep
Deep grief in Athole's tower:
Wondering if sympathy might steep
That sorrow for one hour;
If words of hers might bring relief,
Might mitigate so great a grief;
Or look of hers have power to bless
Her servants, in their sore distress.

The Duke died on January 16, 1864.

The Queen does not mention the Highland Railway at all for over eight years, except for a passing reference, on Friday, 13 October 1865, of '...Ballinluig, where there is a railway station, ...'. There appears to have been another excursion over Highland metals in the intervening years, when, on Friday, 6 September 1872, '...no British sovereign has ever been so far north'. Then, in September 1873, Queen Victoria had a circular excursion from Balmoral, with the train taken from Ballater to Kingussie, and thence to Inverlochy Castle, eventually returning by train from Inverness via Keith. The outward train journey along the southern mainline is described thus:

Tuesday, September 9, 1873

We had our own comfortable train [from Ballater]... by a quarter to one we were at Stanley Junction, where we left the main line from Aberdeen to the south, and turned into the Highland

Railway. Here, alas! the distance became indistinct, the sky grey, and we began fearing for the afternoon. At one we passed the really beautiful valley of Dunkeld, catching a glimpse of the cathedral and the lovely scenery around, which interested Beatrice very much, and made me think of my pleasant visits and excursions thence; then passed opposite St. Colme's, the Duchess's farm, by Dalguise, and saw the large Celtic cross at Logierait, put up to the late Duke of Athole [in 1866]; then Pitlochry; after which we passed through the magnificent Pass of Killiecrankie.... The dull leaden sky which overhung Dunkeld continued, and soon a white veil began to cover the hills, and slight rain came down.

We passed close by Blair, which reminded me much of my sad visit there in 1863, when I came by this same line to visit the late Duke; and I could now see the great improvements made at the Castle [made by the 7th Duke]. From here the railway (running almost parallel with the road by which we went so happily from Dalwhinnie the reverse way in 1861) passes Dalnaspidal Station - a very lonely spot - then up Drumouchter [sic], with Loch Garry and Loch Ericht, fine and wild, but terribly desolate and devoid of woods and habitations, and so veiled by mist and now beating rain as to be seen to but very little advantage. Next comes Dalwhinnie Station, near the inn where we slept in 1861.... At thirty-five minutes past two we reached Kingussie. The station was decorated with flowers, heather, and flags, and the Master of Lovat and Cluny Macpherson were there. We waited till all our things were put in our carriage, and then got out, in heavy rain at that moment...

(Diary of Queen Victoria)

This was Queen Victoria's last journey through Highland Perthshire. The railway itself is merely an adjunct to the story and her feelings about the place, nothing more. That she loved the area is without doubt. We may like to reflect upon these words:

...these dream days in Atholl and Breadalbane were a perfume that sweetened her life to the very end.

A severe close-up, showing three carriage covers. The goods shed is recently built, and behind there are the first four cottages built by the HR for railway workers. The roof line shows they have been extended behind the goods shed – this dates the photo to after 1881 but before 1891 when the foreman's house had been built onto the left of the cottages – this was a far more substantial house with dormers. The chimney pots of the two new cottages sit together in their common wall – just visible above the goods shed's roof ridge; the rightmost stack belongs to the goods shed to warm the goods agent's cubicle just inside the shed itself. *(from GWW B0487, Author's collection)*

Covering The Carriages

The sheeting shown shrouding a carriage in the chapter *Early Days at Blair Athole* was a feature which, to my knowledge, had long slipped from the collective memory of students of the Highland Railway, and no other photographs had previously turned up. What exactly was the purpose of this sheeting? It could be to protect the vehicle, from the snow or the sun, or it could be to conceal the vehicle after an accident or to make it basically weatherproof pending, say, a broken window being repaired.

The 1888 Rule Book clarified things with this entry:

Rule 187: "At Stations where Passenger Plant is kept, the Station Agents are to see the vehicles are always in good order, the windows kept closed, and the ventilators open; that they are always kept under cover, where accommodation is afforded for that purpose, and, where there is no Carriage-shed, that they are covered with sheets to protect them from the sun ...."

This makes clear that the purpose of carriage sheeting was to protect the coach from the depredations of the sun. Not only would the exterior paintwork be vulnerable to fading, its varnish overcoat would need protection from crazing and peeling, and the interior fabrics would also be susceptible to physical damage and fading, as anyone even today can amply testify in their own front room. One photograph shows seven sheeted carriages and is clear enough to make out the lettering. Another photograph shows an eighth sheeted carriage at the far end of the siding (see the chapter Early Days at Blair Athole). Both photographs were taken on the same occasion, probably in early 1880s, but at slightly different times of the day: the former is possibly just the earlier (by a few minutes!). There is another photo, taken at another time, which shows three sheeted coaches.

The two contemporaneous photographs show that one of the two lay-by sidings at Blair Athole has a train of nine four-wheel rib-sided carriages by the northbound platform. There are two other carriages, one sheeted, visible in a short kickback siding beyond the northbound station loop – this is a somewhat odd place to park carriages: there could even be a third coach hidden by the cottage. Of those eleven visible, eight have their sides and at least one end if not both sheeted, and the roofs left uncovered.

From this information, I have prepared two drawings of a carriage sheet showing the two visible styles of lettering, illustrated below.

As far as can be made out, the only unsheeted carriages are two all-thirds and the brake van, all the first or composite class carriages being sheeted. It cannot be determined whether this is significant or not! Perhaps Blair Athole only had an allocation of eight sheets.

Examples of the layout of lettering on one side of a carriage sheet. Not to scale.
(drawings: Howard Geddes)

```
+-----------------------------------+
|          H   R$^Y$   C$^O$        |
|     BLAIR   ATHOLE   ST$^N$       |
|               N$^O$ 2             |
+-----------------------------------+
```

```
+-----------------------------------+
|          HIGHLAND  R$^Y$          |
|     BLAIR   ATHOLE   ST$^N$       |
|               N$^O$ 5             |
+-----------------------------------+
```

Of several sheets that can be read to varying degrees under the magnifying glass, at least two are on upside down. The sheets are identified to the station and are numbered: at Blair Athole, numbers 1, 2 and probably 3 can all be made out. Some are marked "Highland RY"; some have a shorter "H RY CO". They appear to be attached by connecting the edges of the sheet to the external communication cord eyes, which are situated along the top of the sides of the carriages. The fixing has not been executed particularly neatly, the sheets taking on a rather undulating appearance. I cannot make out the actual means of fixing - presumably the sheets have brass eyelets along their edges so they can be tied to the communication cord eyes by short lengths of rope.

The sheets' total size can only be guessed: at around 30 feet per side, they might have been anything up to 76 feet long by 8 feet high. They look white in colour (one looks quite dirty), no doubt to reflect the sun. The colour of the block lettering is unknown, but certainly dark — we might suppose chocolate brown. They are presumably rain-proof, and hence likely to be made of tarpaulin. They must have been quite unwieldy to handle. Arrangements for storage and deployment are not known, although the most obvious place is a store room in the passenger waiting shed on the adjacent northbound platform. These sheets would offer little protection from rain, snow and frost, and only a little protection from driving wind. If the intention was to protect the vehicles from the depredations of the sun, this would be as much to protect the interiors from fading as to protect the outside paint work. I infer that sheeting would be used only for when carriages were to be stored out of use for lengthy periods of time, rather than between regular services and particularly not overnight.

Black Island Platform, looking south, 21 June 1957. The platform face is in fair condition although the surface is heavily overgrown. *(J L Stevenson, courtesy Hamish Stevenson)*

Summer Camps at Black Island

Around 1900, in South Africa during the Boer War, Lord Tullibardine took command of a regiment raised from Scotsmen living in that country. Called The Scottish Horse, by February 1901 it was four squadrons strong. A second regiment was raised from volunteers in Scotland and Australia, and both regiments fought with distinction throughout the war.

Returning to Scotland, Lord Tullibardine raised two new Yeomanry regiments of The Scottish Horse: 1st Regiment recruited from Perthshire, 2nd Regiment from Aberdeenshire, Elgin, Nairn and Argyllshire.

And what has this to do with The Highland Railway? Well, Lord Tullibardine became the Duke Of Atholl. The Scottish Horse, as volunteer Yeomanry, came together in a summer camp once a year, rather as the Territorials today must train together once a year. The summer camp was regularly held on Black Island which is a tract of land a mile west of Blair Castle and is right beside the Highland main line not far from Blair Atholl Station.

And they all arrived by train ....

Black Island. Part of the Atholl Estate, Black Island is a generally flat expanse of grassy land between the River Garry and the Highland mainline - see the map. I don't know the origins of the name. In effect, Black Island was the bottom of the Duke's back garden, and the new Inverness & Perth Junction Railway passed right through, cutting Black Island off from Blair Castle. There is evidence that an avenue used to lead from the Castle straight down to the river at Black Island.

Summer Camps at Black Island. The first camp at Blair Atholl was in the summer of 1904. The postcard on page 99 shows a view from the lineside, which appears to be of that first camp because the postcard is annotated, presumably by the sender, "2 July 1904". Unfortunately, the extremely clear postmark has been mostly destroyed with the removal of the stamp; it was clearly posted in Blair Atholl, to Miss Sime in Murthly from "WB".

Black Island Platform. Such was the anticipated extent of the rail traffic, the Highland Railway agreed on 26 April 1904 to provide a special Platform for the "Scottish Horse Encampment". Hence, Black Island Platform was quickly built and brought into service in time for that first camp a couple of months later. I do not know the precise date of opening. We can assume

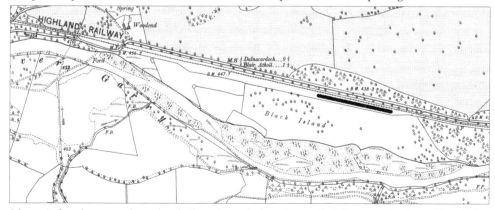

I haven't found a map where the platform is marked so I've marked its approximate position. Being surveyed in 1898, this shows a single line instead of the double line in place in 1904. The level crossing adjacent to the platform can be seen.   (National Library of Scotland)

that it was simply built ready for the first camp; the opening date can best be regarded as the day on which it was first used by the Scottish Horse, presumably some days before the camp started in mid-June, in order to prepare for the influx.

The Platform was situated only on the Down side, 36m 16ch from Perth, precisely 1333 yards west of Blair Atholl North Box. It was never publicly advertised, but was announced as being closed to passengers as late as 11 April 1959. I do not know when it was demolished, nor what became of the remains. The photo was taken 21 June 1957, when the remains of the cookhouse, ablutions and suchlike installations still existed on the site. There was a Forestry Commission house at the level crossing, which was manned until the Forestry Commission closed their sleeping accommodation in 1950; the Army then got a key to let themselves in. No.5 Company, Canadian Forestry Corps had their camp there between 26 December 1940 and 1 April 1944, but it's not entirely clear to what extent if any rail was used over road for the transportation of the timber. An inspection visit had this to report: "road and rail transport for [Canadian Forestry Corps'] sawn lumber are available practically beside the mill. Lt.-Col. Jones remarked however he would be better pleased if the British authorities made greater use of these facilities to remove the lumber, instead of letting it accumulate at the spot where it is produced".

Operating Arrangements. As implied above, trains came from all over, all on a single day. Therefore, the purpose of this chapter is to describe the special arrangements put into effect at Blair Atholl for the "invasion". I have drawn mostly on the Highland Railway's Weekly Notice for Saturday 13th June 1914.

First, the preparation:

BLACK ISLAND PLATFORM BETWEEN BLAIR-ATHOLL AND
STRUAN FOR SCOTTISH HORSE CAMP.

Until further notice, this Platform will be used for Camp Traffic only, and worked from Blair-Atholl. Trains to be worked from Blair-Atholl to the Platform and back on Down Line of Rails. For this purpose the Down Starting Signal at Blair-Atholl will be bolt-locked from North Cabin with Key bearing label

```
        Blair-Atholl
             and
    Black Island Platform
```

which must be carried by Engine-driver of every Train working to and from the Platform.

Stationmaster, Blair-Atholl, *to arrange for Special Trains working to and from Platform as required, and when such can be done without delay to ordinary Trains, sending a weekly return to this Office of trips made.*

Level Crossing Gates *are situated at South End and Wicket Gates for Foot Passengers at North End of Platform, and, when required, will be under charge of Gateman. Drivers of all Engines must sound their Whistles when approaching, and keep a sharp lookout for Signals.* **Return Pilot Engines to reduce speed to 3 miles an hour when passing Platform.**

This last paragraph pinpoints the Platform's site precisely: the Level Crossing is marked on the 1898 and 1966 Ordnance Surveys, and I believe still exists.

The Weekly Notice also states:

Loco Dept, Blair-Atholl, *to supply an Engine to work Trains to and from Camp Platform. Perth Engines to be turned and ready to attach to Empty Trains immediately on arrival, from Camp Platform, at Blair-Atholl.*

(The terminating trains) to return Empty from Blair-Atholl to Perth when ready, and as Line will admit without delay to Ordinary Trains. All Cal. [Caledonian Railway] Stock to be handed over at Perth.

Ian Scrimgeour noted in 1936 that when the Key mentioned above was withdrawn it locked the lever at Danger and its possession by the driver gave him authority to pass the Advanced Starter at Danger; and that when the train had served the platform it could return Wrong Line to Blair North Signal Box. Also, the train was signalled to Struan but when it returned that was cancelled. The mode of operation was most probably that the train engine would be replaced by the local engine, which would draw the train forward to the Platform. After everyone and everything had detrained, the train would be pushed wrong-line back to Blair Atholl. There are a variety of possibilities for the train engine rejoining the train ready for return southwards. One is that the train engine waits at the Up Starter and the local engine pushes the whole train through a crossover by the North Box to buffer up. Another is that the train halts by the North Box and the train engine couples on and pulls the train from the down to the up line. Another is that the train is propelled into one of the three available lay-bys, until a departure slot can be found. Although there was never any accident or incident as far as we know, there was every opportunity for irregular workings or conflicting movements within the confines of the Advanced Starter – presumably everyone was expected to be vigilant, with the requisite degree of bawling, shouting and hand waving to achieve safe working. The one starter signal on the left at the end of the platform governed all three or latterly all four lay-bys, and the practice when there were two or more trains waiting was indeed for the signalman to gesticulate from his cabin to indicate which train had the authority to depart and which didn't. What manner of gesticulation, both by the signalman and the driver in response, whether by arrangement or for other reasons, isn't known although one North Box signalman averred that orders had to be carried by word-of-mouth from the signalman to the driver to avoid confusion, which was more genteel than in actual fact.

I do not have details of what happened when the Camp ended. Presumably, the reverse of the above. A hint is given in the LMS 1937 Appendix, which states-

> From: Black Island Platform
> To: Blair Atholl North
> On: Down Line (Northbound)
> "Military Traffic from Camp, *including vehicles containing passengers in wrong direction*. Only when specifically authorised in fortnightly notice." (My underlining.)

This suggests that the local engine still pulled the (empty) train to the Platform and propelled the (full) train down to Blair Atholl North. Maybe then the train engine took charge and pulled the train over from the down to the up line.

The Special Trains. Now to details of the trains themselves. Saturday 13th June 1914 was an extremely busy day on the Highland, with many extra passenger trains.

First, there was a Guaranteed Excursion from Dundee to Pitlochry, Kingussie and Inverness, coming through Blair Atholl 8.39am. An hour later, along came two Nobels' Factory Workers' Excursion trains, en route from Ardrossan to Inverness. The probable number of excursionists is given as 1000, and it is noted that a third train may be necessary. These three, possibly four, trains caused three goods trains to be shunted at various places, with two of those being shunted twice. A fourth train took 400 of Keiller & Sons employees from Dundee to Dunkeld, arriving at 10.10am.

And then it got busy...

In all, eight trains arrived throughout the afternoon and evening, all but one of which had to be taken up to Black Island and back again. This obviously blocked the Down line for a significant amount of time. Just check what had to be unloaded, and one realises that it was not a five-minute job. The disruption to normal service trains must have been great, especially if they themselves were being run in more than one portion.

All then had to return empty, finding paths back as best they could. It does not take much to imagine that the later arriving trains would be crossing the earlier returning trains somewhere between Blair Atholl and Stanley. And quite likely the later returning trains would be interweaving with the returning Excursion trains.

The details are quite fascinating, so I will extensively quote from the Highland Notice. Unless mentioned otherwise, all the following trains are bringing The Scottish Horse to Black Island Platform.

Special Train No:		6	1	7	8	5	9	10	11
Perth	dep:	12.05p		1.40	2.55	3.00	4.15	5.07	6.00
Elgin	dep:		9.40a						
Blair-Atholl	arr:	1.50p	2.50p	3.40	4.20	4.28	6.10	6.50	7.43

Train No 6: Mixed Train with Aberdeen Squadron. Engine and Guard light from Perth, to take train from Cal Co at Stanley at 12.25pm.

Train No 1: Consisted of
    1 Brake Composite,
    2 Third Class Carriages
    1 Luggage Van
    1 Goods Brake Van
    4 Horse boxes (approx)
    13 Cattle Trucks (approx)

a total of around 22 vehicles. This train started at Elgin and picked up men and Horse Boxes and Cattle Trucks, en route. The anticipated arrangements were:

Elgin (proper)	- 41 Men, 1 Horse Box, 5 Cattle Trucks
Elgin (off GNS ex Cullen)	- 15 Men, 2 Cattle Trucks
Forres	- 9 Men, 2 Cattle Trucks
Grantown-on-Spey	- 3 Horses
Boat of Garten (off Speyside)	- 32 Men, 4 Cattle Trucks

No operating arrangements are mentioned for this train. One can assume that it passed Black Island on the Up line without stopping, and into Blair Atholl. The likeliest thing to happen then would be that the Train would be handled just like the ex-Perth trains, being taken to and from the Platform by the local engine whilst the train engine turned, coaled and watered ready for the return journey empty, past the Platform yet again.

Train No 7: Mixed Train with Perth Squadron. 140 Horses in Cattle Trucks, 11 Horses in Boxes (the Officers'!), and accommodation for 4 officers and 90 men. Will pick up a few Trucks Horses at Stanley, also 12 men 9 horses in Trucks, 1 Horsebox and 1 Truck Baggage at Dunkeld.

In addition, 31 Men, 2 Horse Boxes and Van Baggage from Alyth and Couper-Angus to be picked up at Stanley.

Train No 8: Mixed Train with Callander and District Squadron from Cal Co, including

	Horsebox from Methven, 15-16 Vehicles. Will lift a few Vehicles from Stanley if required.
	In addition, 5/6 Cattle Trucks with Horses from Blairgowrie and Couper-Angus to be picked up at Stanley.
Train No 5:	This is the one train not terminating at Blair Atholl. It follows immediately behind Train 8, and is not related to the Scottish Horse movements. Instead, it is taking the Army Service Corps from Perth to Kingussie, departing Blair Atholl at 4.31 having stopped for the collection of Tickets. I presume that Train 8, having arrived at 4.20, would be held in a lay-by at Blair Atholl whilst Train 5 overtakes, although the timetable does not show this.
	This train to carry 1 Officer, 50 Men, 15 Horses in Cattle Trucks, and 6 Transport Wagons in Fish Trucks. Due to arrive Kingussie 5.55pm.
Train No 9:	Mixed Train with Aberdeen Squadron. The second such train, with the same arrangements as Train 6.
Train No 10:	Mixed Train with Gourock Squadron from Cal Co. 9 Vehicles.
Train No 11:	Mixed Train with Argyll Squadron from Cal Co. 13-14 Vehicles. The 5.20pm down goods to be shunted at Dunkeld for Train 11 to pass.

As mentioned above, Trains 6, 7, 8, 9, 10, 11 all to return to Perth empty, as soon as practicable, with Trains 10 and 11 coupled together. There are no timings for any of the returning Special Trains, although some certainly returned same-day. So we can infer a heavy session of returning tired-but-happy excursionists mid to late evening.

But that's not all. A couple of normal service trains were used to bring men and their impedimenta to camp, as follows:

12 noon Down Passenger:	70 Men and Horse Box from Dundee, also 1 Horse Box each from Errol, Crieff and Comrie.
12.25pm Down Goods:	7/8 Cattle Trucks with Horses from Dundee.

A postcard showing the Scottish Horse encamped at Blair Atholl - the railway embankment can be seen bottom left corner. (Author's Collection)

Post Script. To round off, the Army Service Corps were clearly on the move that day. In addition to Train 5 Perth-Kingussie, there was another Train departing 12.01pm from Edderton of all places to Kingussie. For the record, this consisted of a First-class Saloon, 6 Thirds and a Brake-Third, the stock having arrived empty by yet another special train from Inverness that morning. It was augmented at Tain by a further Compo, 3 Thirds and Passenger Brake Van, off yet another special that had brought Army Service Corps from Inverness to Tain that morning. It's not clear whether these coaches were simply hitching a lift empty back to Inverness, or were loaded to Kingussie.

One train included 9 Fish Trucks with Folding Sides and 1 ordinary Fish Truck. I wonder why the subtle distinction?

As a matter of interest, the Fife and Forfar Yeomanry, with whom The Scottish Horse would amalgamate in later years, started their summer camp at Tain the previous day. Four trains, one for each of their squadrons, had come through Blair Atholl en route that day.

Finally, the Army Service Corps had another special converging on Kingussie, leaving Kyle at 10.30am with 1 Compo, 6 Thirds and Brake, that stock having also come up from Inverness earlier that morning.

Conclusion. Thus ends to story of the Scottish Horse's arrival from all points of Scotland at Blair Atholl that day. It is likely that this happened in much the same way in other years. The Camps continued at least into the 1930s, as evidenced by a photograph of the Duke of Atholl addressing the men at Black Island under Tulach Hill around 1934.

As for The Scottish Horse itself, a third regiment was added at the outbreak of the Great War; only a couple of months later The Scottish Horse became a brigade under Brigadier Lord Tullibardine. They fought in Gallipoli and Egypt. A battalion, as part of the Black Watch, fought in Salonika and the Western Front.

The Scottish Horse retained a horsed role as scouts until December 1939, when they converted to artillery. They were active in various roles throughout World War II.

After that war, they reformed as a regiment of the Royal Armoured Corps. In 1956, they amalgamated with the Fife and Forfar Yeomanry and were renamed the Highland Yeomanry in 1969. When this article was originally written [1993], it was then represented by 239 (Highland Yeomanry) Squadron, RCT(V) (Royal Corps of Transport - Volunteer).

Inspection parade at Black Island. The platform is in the background.
(Author's collection)

THE VISIT OF CROWN PRINCE HIROHITO

Crown Prince Hirohito and his entourage visited Blair Castle on Saturday 21st May 1921 for a few days. He came by special train, although he left that at Perth and travelled onward by car in a cavalcade, with the train making its way separately to Blair Atholl with the party's luggage.

In early 1921 the Foreign Office asked the eighth Duke and Duchess of Atholl (known to each other as 'Bardie' and 'Kitty') if they would host an especially important visitor, the Crown Prince of Japan. The Duke and Duchess prepared carefully, drilling the Atholl Highlanders and polishing the castle and its contents. Sheila Hetherington (in *Katharine Atholl, 1874- 1960, Against the Tide*) describes how one problem was solved:

"One of the ghillies was found to have such large feet that none of the regulation [Atholl Highlander] buckled brogues would fit him. Bardie thought that it would be a pity to leave him out on that account, so the toes were cut off the largest pair available, leaving his stockinged feet protruding. It was considered that the Crown Prince would be too pleased by the entire spectacle to notice: the Atholl Highlanders on parade are an impressive body of men."

On his way to Blair Atholl, Hirohito passed through Dunkeld, and two children, one from Dunkeld School and the other from Birnam, presented him with bouquets. The Duke's brother, Lord James Murray ('Hamish') wrote his sister about some of the arrangements:

They arrived on the 21st [of May] and Bardie and I went down to Perth to meet them. Their special train arrived at 1:35. A guard of honour of the Black Watch was drawn up in front of the Station Hotel, and various Perth dignitaries were presented. Then the whole party started off in motor cars for Blair.

On arrival at Blair we stopped a few moments outside the front lodge where a crowd had assembled; Macdonald of the Inn made a suitable speech, and we continued on to the Castle in front of which was drawn up a Guard of Honour of Atholl Highlanders commanded by Edradynate, Young Fergusson of Baledmund and Charlie Butter carrying the colours ...

What Hamish didn't mention was that Bardie's plan for a 21-gun salute had misfired, and the prince had been greeted by a single-gun salute. Sheila Hetherington notes: "His Imperial Highness, being happily unaware of the intention to provide a further twenty, was delighted by this triumphant welcome."

This raises the question why they would travel by car rather than in the special train – presumably nothing more complicated than to show the county to the visitors and the visitors to the county. The issued instructions were clear: "The Special Train, servants, and baggage, after His Imperial Highness has detrained at Perth, will proceed to Blair Atholl, where a motor lorry has been detailed to meet the train for conveyance of baggage at 2.35pm". The train stayed there in the sidings for the full length of their visit, over three nights: not only does the itinerary show this, but it has been stated that "the staff of his imperial suite slept in the special train in a siding at Blair Atholl". Maybe the train was stabled there only for accommodation purposes, and that Hirohito travelled back to Perth by car. I wonder what was the train's consist?

Hamish continues with the formal story of the Saturday they arrived:

The Prince inspected the Guard and he and Prince Kan-in were then conducted to the front door where they were received with a beautiful curtsey from Kitty. Inside the Front Hall were assembled the House Party who were presented. They comprised, Marjorie MacKenzie, Locheil and Lady Hermione Cameron, Walter Fotheringham and wife, Ferelith Rattray and husband, Charlie Butter and wife, Mrs. and Miss Anstruther Gray, Miss McEwen, Douglas Ramsay, and Uncle Bob, Bill and Gwen Moray came in place of the Butters on the Monday.

The Crown Prince had the Red room, which has latterly been painted pale grey and now has a bathroom attached. The Derby room was his sitting room. Prince Kan-in was given the Banvie room, which now contains the old Derby room furniture, which was bought for Queen Victoria.

That evening Bardie took the princes up to one of the fishing pools in Glen Tilt, and there is more surviving descriptions of the visit. The Prince remembered the visit so vividly he asked to come back again when he visited Britain in 1938. Despite the looming war and times of economic stringency on the estate, the second visit was carried off with just as much success as the first.

The party at the Castle impressed the Japanese because the atmosphere was so informal that local villagers were allowed to mingle casually with the aristocracy, and made all the more memorable by an incongruous rendition of Japan's national anthem "Kimi ga yo" on the bagpipes, and made positively unforgettable by toasts to the Crown Prince with the usual Highland honours of guests standing with one foot on the table, which in turn so impressed the Japanese that they also stood on chairs and "Banzaied". A newspaper reported of their cordial farewells when Prince Hirohito's party arrived at the station after midnight. Many must have experienced the 5.00am departure next day with a heavy head.

The itinerary of the Hirohito special train was issued by the Foreign Office as follows [PRO FO/371/6691]. There will also be special train notices issued by the Highland Railway, although none seem to have survived. However a copy of the detailed arrangements for the car cavalcade from Perth to Blair Atholl along with the associated train movement has survived.

Wednesday 18th May 1921	09 00 depart Chesterfield House for King's Cross
	09 30 depart King's Cross
	10 52 arrive Cambridge
	The day is to be spent touring various colleges etc
	23 10 depart Cambridge for Edinburgh
Thursday 19th May 1921	08 00 breakfast served on train
	09 30 arrive Waverley Station, Edinburgh
	Rest of day touring Edinburgh
Friday 20th May 1921	11 35 depart Waverley for Rosyth
	13 00 arrive Rosyth
	Tour of Rosyth
	16 00 depart Rosyth - afternoon tea served on train
	18 00 arrive Waverley
Saturday 21st May 1921	12 00 depart Waverley for Blair Atholl
	14 35 arrive Blair Atholl
	Stay at Blair Castle
Tuesday 24th May 1921	05 00 depart Blair Atholl
	- breakfast - lunch - afternoon tea served on train
	15 00 arrive Manchester
	Stay in Manchester
Thursday 26th May 1921	15 00 depart Manchester - afternoon tea served on train
	19 10 arrive King's Cross.

The Loading Gauge

There was a minor structure at practically every station in Britain called a Loading Gauge. Its function was to make sure that loads in wagons did not exceed the maximum dimensions applicable to the line. There had to be sufficient clearance for wagons to pass safely under bridges and through tunnels and to clear lineside structures such as signals and telegraph poles, not to mention other trains passing on adjacent lines. Open wagons in particular could be loaded with bulky but relatively light substances, for example hay and straw; there are photographs of wagons whose tarpaulin covering sheets were positively ballooning with whatever was underneath, such that one wonders whether loading dimensions were more observed in their breach. Nevertheless, a Loading Gauge had an express purpose.

The loading gauge in 1963. Motor cars would have been driven along the goods yard on the right and around the ramp up on to the grassy platform. Blair Atholl North Cabin is in the background. (Howard Geddes)

When I first carried out a photographic survey of Blair Atholl back in 1963, I noticed a feature which puzzled me for many years. I have faithfully recreated it in model form, and I have not been backward in being forward pointing out the strangeness to visitors. And this puzzle? The placing of the Loading Gauge beyond the far end of the loading bank at Blair Atholl within yards of the buffer stops, as though, like one of Tolkien's trees, it had somehow walked its way away from the Goods Shed and the Yard Crane after an argument with them. Why sulk at the end of a siding, uselessly inaccessible behind any waiting wagons?

There did appear to be the capability for end-loading, a ramp of sorts twisting around from the goods yard, squeezed between the sidings' end and the Banvie Burn. But, so?

The answer, as so often, arrived without notice, by chance, and many years later. In the depths of an HR Official Guide, on page 191, was this fascinating offering:

HIGHLAND MOTOR NOTES.

On account of the bad road which leads into the Highlands by the Pass of Drumochter, many motorists have been deterred from enjoying the good roads and the beautiful scenery which are to be found North of Inverness. The Highland Railway Company, far from wishing to drive motors out of the Highlands, have shown both good sense and enterprise in the offer they make to motor parties to convey motor cars by rail from Blair-Atholl to Inverness, thus avoiding the bad road, at extremely low rates; and also to issue tickets at specially reduced fares to passengers accompanying their cars on the journey. The ordinary rate for motor cars from Blair-Atholl to Inverness is 48/5 (owner's risk) by passenger train, and the Highland Company now offer to convey them for the charge of 30/- for each car (owner's risk); the ordinary single passenger fare for this journey is First Class, 13/9; and Third Class, 6/10½; and the reduced fares for motor parties accompanying their motors is now to be First Class, 10/-; and Third Class, 5/-.

These very substantial reductions should of themselves attract motor parties to the "Further North," and are also well worthy of attention in view of the great saving to tyres, which seldom survive a run over the Dalnaspidal road.

The light dawned: how else to load the motor cars other than by using the ramp at the end of the siding? How else to ensure that the Rolls-Royce will not bang into bridges than by The Loading Gauge?

But were there not carriage trucks that were covered? Ah yes, but they were extra! On the inside front cover of the Guide there is this:

IMPORTANT NOTICE TO MOTORISTS *VISITING THE HIGHLANDS OF SCOTLAND.*

During June, July and August, in order that Motor Cars may avoid traversing the rough roads over the Grampians, and consequent liability of damage to tyres, the Highland Railway Company are prepared to convey Motor Cars from Blair-Atholl to Inverness by any ordinary passenger train, except the early morning trains or 11.50 a.m. ex Perth, at the specially reduced rate of 30/- each, owner's risk, plus usual charges for covered truck when such is used.

Motor parties accompanying their Cars will be conveyed from Blair-Atholl to Inverness at the cheap single journey fares of First Class, 10/-; and Third Class, 5/-.

That extra is charged for covered trucks necessarily means that extra is not charged for open trucks – so presumably those open trucks built by the Highland Railway for horse-drawn carriages before the coming of the motor car were available and were intended for use at Blair Atholl for motor cars. And of course, if motor cars were loaded to go up by rail, then motor cars would come down by rail and be unloaded. Now I have a reason-to-be for The Loading Gauge.

This shows how close it was to the end of the siding. It was only when I was messing about with the local merchant's coal wagons on my model layout of Blair Atholl that it dawned upon me the reason for that opening which, if a window, is in the most odd position. It's a coal hole! Exactly the right height for shovelling the coal out of the wagon into its storage shed. The wagon's drop-down door or just planks can be rested on the horizontal batten. There were a couple of other similar sheds at Blair Atholl - never intended to be glazed, just as well I modelled them as I found them. It is only today when I studied the photo in close-up, that I realised the opening has a door! Notice also, by the way, metal keys on the main line, wooden keys on the sidings (and the crossover in the foreground). (Howard Geddes)

The guide cited above is, in full, the *Official A.B.C. Tourist Guide To The Highlands Of Scotland Via The Highland Railway* by T.A. Wilson, General Manager, a substantial 200 page affair giving everything anybody wanted to know, from fares to ferries, from tickets to tours. But it has one misprint that rather surprised me – persistently on every map accompanying its Circular Tours is the station of Bair Atholl! The Guide is undated but is probably 1908, for the Highland Railway trumpets its 'newest type of carriage' which is a corridor composite coach, that pictured being No. 12 which was built by Brush in 1908.

I have never come across mention of this service before, and I cannot recall any photographs of vehicles on carriage trucks south of Inverness, although I'd be happy to be corrected on this. It strikes me that the chances of motor vehicles fouling the loading gauge would actually be slight (unless luggage was loaded high on their roof racks), but the same might not be said of horse-drawn carriages. And this raised of course the further question of the accompanying horse having to be given a lift too.

This leads us to ask when this end-loading facility was built? None of the intuitive answers is the right - e.g. line opening, line doubling, the coming of the motor car. No, the structure was slightly built out into the Banvie Burn, the OS map makes that clear. It had already been built by 1892, because it clearly shows on plans dated thus for a proposed remodelling of the station. But it was not there in 1884 when a plan was drawn showing a sliver of land given by the Duke of Athole to the HR, being the site of the then-unbuilt second southbound lay-by siding on the other side of the Banvie Burn.

The original end-loading bay. The end of the goods-yard kickback siding in 1963. End-loading was clearly capable here at one time. But the platform was first narrowed (could only have been to extend the Station Master's garden behind) and then reinstated with a fairly substantial wooden building containing Boiler and Lamp Room facilities which lasted well through LMS times. The building in the photo seems to have been at least equal oldest in the whole station. It suddenly disappeared around 2010 - I don't suppose anyone knew about its pedigree. (Howard Geddes)

This 1884-1892 period wasn't even when end-loading was first introduced, for that 1884 plan has a rather interesting feature that looks suspiciously like an end-loading facility straight from the station platform to the Goods Shed kickback siding – the photo on page 105 shows clearly where it was. Only by reviewing in the light of this the 1898 OS and the later LMS rating plans, can one see that end-loading was no longer a practical proposition, because there was no longer enough space to manoeuvre vehicles on the platform even if the track were still in situ. Thus, for whatever reason end-loading was moved from one end of the goods yard to the other sometime between 1884 and 1892. Indeed the very earliest OS map of 1867 shows that platform-end end-loading must have been there since the railway was first built even though there seems to be a signal-post in danger of getting in the way (and a photograph confirms that this was before the goods shed was built). I'll put that down to slack drawing – there is a far-worse more-glaring error very nearby where an entire crossover has been omitted!

Thus an interesting long-forgotten example of railway service has re-emerged from the scantiest of evidence.

The main line over Drumochter, where the small stone in remembrance of Jimmy Stewart nestles unnoticed from passing trains. The story is related in the next chapter.
(Howard Geddes)

A Fateful Hogmanay

A railwayman's life was never easy, with many men working long and arduous hours for their employer: it cost some their lives. This tale is about one incident. There are no morals to be drawn and no feats of heroism to be described. But perhaps the story provides an insight into the life and times of the ordinary people who worked the railways.

What I'm going to recount happened in 1921. Other dates - 1923, 1924 or 1932 - have been given, but I believe the earlier date is right, for reasons I'll show later on. The facts have echoed down the years, and in so doing have become blurred, transformed through memory and half-telling. When I first heard this story, around 1996, there were those still alive who remembered what happened, and so I put on record what I believe to be the real story, before the underlying facts are lost forever.

This story is about Jimmy Stewart. He was a surfaceman on the Gourach section of the line, which is near the top of The Hill by Dalnaspidal. Better known as Jimmy Steelie, he was married with three boys and two girls, and the family was known as the Steelies. They lived in one of the block of four railway houses at Altnagourach (or Aultnagourach or Auchnagourach or even Allt Chaorach, depending on who you talk to), a mile and a half south of Dalnaspidal, just north of the second bridge under the railway, on the left going down the hill. These houses have completely gone now, their site being under the A9; their stones but not their soul now form the foundation of the road, at the old summit lay-by at Drumochter, by a peat bog there known as "the hole".

But the story is about what happened on Saturday, December 31st, 1921. In those days, of course, it was the New Year that was celebrated rather than Christmas, and Jimmy was in Pitlochry for the day, doing some shopping. He bought a toy for each of his family. His second child, James, was around 10 years old at the time. He also answered to Hamish, but his real nickname was "Ting-a-ling", or "Ting" for short: this was because of his incessant ringing of his bicycle bell as a toddler! So, we can see that Jimmy had five young children, and the toys were their special treat. It is also relevant to wonder whether Jimmy obtained other gifts, of a liquid nature, and whether he sampled them extensively before being satisfied that the old year could be seen out in an appropriately cheerful and benign manner.

Jimmy caught the afternoon passenger from Perth, which stopped at Pitlochry at 4.40pm according to the 1922 timetable. It is likely the train took on a pilot engine at Blair Atholl, at the same time overtaking the daily Loco Coal train which would be waiting in one of the sidings there. The train continued up the hill, with the pilot coming off at Dalnaspidal, the booked time being 5.40pm. It may be that Jimmy rode on the pilot engine from Blair Atholl, even though the train itself was booked to stop at Dalnaspidal anyway. Having alighted, Jimmy decided to walk the mile and a half back down the hill to Altnagourach, rather than get a lift on the returning pilot. Why he walked along the railway line rather than the road, which was handier, we shall never know. For some reason, he didn't or couldn't hitch a lift on the pilot when it returned down the hill. What he did do was to phone his wife from the signal cabin to get supper ready.

He started to walk down. It was dark. When he didn't appear home in due course, the alarm went out, and a search took place. Jimmy's body was found at the line-side, unmarked bar a graze on the forehead. The two who found him, Bob Wilson, the ganger, and a man called Morrison, took the body home on the permanent-way trolley.

What had happened? Well, here we have a mystery. I have two equally authoritative versions. One that he was killed by the pilot engine returning light down the hill; and the other that he was hit by a goods train coming up the hill following the passenger. This latter train would have been the loco-coal train, due to pass Dalnaspidal around 6.10pm: it was headed by Big Goods No. 108. These were the only two movements around that time, and either is as likely as the other. Probably he was laden with presents, perhaps he had had one "nippie-sweetie" too many; for sure, he could not have heard or seen the approaching locomotive. This suggests that it was the returning pilot that, going downhill, came up behind with a closed regulator and brought a mere glancing yet fatal blow to the man trudging along beside the track, absorbed in anticipating the night's celebrations.

His fellow workmen erected a small memorial on the site, near milepost 50, which was on the widest embankment on the Highland Railway according to Murdo Dryden who was a ganger at Blair Atholl. The simple memorial was a sleeper set upright in the ground at the exact spot, shaped rather as a milepost with rounded top, and with "James Stewart" and "31-12-21" carved into it. Some of the gangers looked after it, but eventually it disappeared, maybe buried under old ballast, or more likely just rotted away. Murdo Dryden remembers re-sleepering at that point in 1932 and seeing the sleeper monument "much decayed". Willie Duncan can remember, as a p-way inspector on the Kingussie District 1945-1955, seeing a piece of the sleeper in the ground near the 50 mile post.

What became of the family? They were destitute. Bob Wilson and other colleagues did everything that they could for them but Mother was still faced with a hard time bringing up the five children: there was no pay, no insurance, nothing in those days. Even worse, the family had to leave their railway cottage. They were a Perthshire family, and they were able to move to a small house at Pitagowan, which is right beside the railway between Bruar and Calvine.

The eldest son, Donald, worked on the Struan section with Murdo Dryden: "a good worker and nice fellow". Eventually he left the railway over some kind of a dispute with his superiors.

Ting got a job on Bruar Farm as a teenager for 3 years, then became a porter at Struan and worked his way up the ranks to become signalman at Brodie then Dalcross. He returned to Dalnaspidal as relief signalman at Blair Atholl. Norman Alderman, the signalman at Dalnaspidal, got to know Ting well. Ting died in Pitlochry's hospital about 1976.

I know little about Johnnie, the third son, and nothing about the two girls, although it seems that they never married.

Now, when I first came across this story, it was about Ting Stewart, as though he were the signalman at Dalnaspidal (the "ting" being supposed that of the block bells, not that of a child's bicycle!), and it was he who got run over; the accident was dated as 1932, and December 31st 1932 is indeed a Saturday. Furthermore, the memorial sleeper became a memorial stone. I am now reasonably confident that the story I have related is right, yet I still have some doubts: the alternative date given was 1923 or 1924 and neither has the 31st as a Saturday, hence my stated date of 1921. This fits with Ting, who died around 1976, being born around 1911. His contemporaries were also born around that time. As a final rebuttal of the 1932 date, No. 108, one of the engines stated as being involved, was scrapped in 1930.

The photograph on page 106, taken in 1996 and looking north with The Sow of Atholl at Drumochter in the background, shows the place, as far as I can tell. There is a permanent-way hut opposite but this was built long afterwards. Just by the birch tree on the right lay a little boulder, the only one around - you can just see it lying in the cess. I set it upright, a small act of remembrance of the day a railwayman died as he took home to his children their New Year toys.

ACKNOWLEDGEMENTS

My first visit to Blair Atholl was in May 1963, cheap plastic camera at the ready, still at school but just passed the driving test, with car for the 1000 mile round trip borrowed from astonishingly understanding parents. I have been researching Blair Atholl's railway in fits and starts for nigh on fifty years, albeit with long gaps due to family and career commitments and the sheer distance from home. The primary purpose of my research was to build a model railway layout of Blair Atholl: this has been achieved and is all the more satisfying with an understanding of the history and background of the area. My thanks to:-

Jane Anderson, Archivist, Blair Castle. I have thoroughly plundered the Archives of all railway related material. Without Jane's enthusiastic assistance, this book wouldn't exist. Reproduction of several illustrations from the Archives is by permission.

John Cameron, for his foresight and energy in gathering such an extensive collection of railway material for the Atholl Country Life Museum. Reproduction of their material is courtesy of Atholl Country Life Museum.

Re Summer Camps at Black Island: Dr Patrick Mileham, for sending me all the relevant extracts from his book; also to the Scottish Horse Museum in Dunkeld.

Re The Visit Of Crown Prince Hirohito: the late Nancy Cameron, who used to own the Atholl Browse bookshop, for permission to quote copiously from her write-up of the visit.

Re Blair Atholl's Water Supply: the Gordon family, Lude Estate, for access to estate papers; Alistair Stephen, Lude keeper, for taking the time, at short notice and between deer shoots, to show me around; the bloke from Scottish Water who stopped digging his hole to pass the time of day (and to moan about the lousy plans causing him to dig many fruitless holes in the ground searching for old pipes, before they gave it up as a lost cause).

Also John Burns, then of Milton of Kincraigie, for allowing me access to the Loco Shed which he owned, and spending a good deal of time hunting around in the old lay-by sidings looking for 'Tobies' – the valves at the junctions of pipes - still in use supplying his Loco Shed and the Station as well as various workmen's and estate cottages in the old goods yard, and the Back Lodge across the old A9. We wondered at the impossibility of ever turning the water off in the event of a leak: the one valve we found was battered and irretrievably bent but obviously still water tight; the other valves were lost, apparently ignored and buried under decades of ballast and alterations to the sidings. It is probably just as well that we never did find the cesspits that served the railside block of toilets that survived for decades outside Blair Atholl's Goods Shed and the lean-to privies that snuggled up to one of the water tanks.

Re The Final Trip Home which first appeared in the Highland Railway *Journal*: John Roake.

Re A Fateful Hogmanay: John Kerr of Old Struan, for first telling me about the story; Norman Alderman, retired signalman who lived by the lineside at Dalnaspidal; John Kennedy, stalker at Dalnaspidal for the past 45 years, and Murdo Dryden of Pitlochry, retired p-way inspector at Inverness, for their recollections; Willie Duncan, ex-p-way inspector for Kingussie District 1945-55, for Murdo's story.

Highland Council Archive department, for access to their depositions, in particular D862/C/1/a Highland Railway Project Estimates 1910-1913. I was allowed to photograph each relevant page, so I could analyse the info at my leisure.

REFERENCE SOURCES

The following are some specific documents I have consulted:

Old Grampian Highways: Comyn's Road & Minigaig Pass, John Kerr F.S.A. (Scot.), 1977

Wade In Atholl, John Kerr F.S.A. (Scot.), 1988

Water Mills of Atholl, John Kerr F.S.A. (Scot.), 1990

Inverness Lawyer And His Sons 1796-1878, Isabel Harriet Anderson, Aberdeen, 1900

Perth & Inverness Prospectus 1845 (also reported in the Perthshire Advertiser 10-4-1845)

The Perth And Inverness Railway : Its Importance as a National and Commercial Enterprise, J. B. Fraser, Esq, of Relig, Inverness-shire, London, 1846.

Reminiscences Of My Life In The Highlands Vol 1 and Vol 2, Joseph Mitchell, 1883 and 1884

Queen Victoria's Highland Journals, ed David Duff, Lomond Books, 1994

Queen Victoria's Scottish Diaries, John Kerr, Eric Dobby Publishing, 1992

Highland Railway Liveries, Howard Geddes & Eddie Bellass, Pendragon & HMRS, 1995

The Yeomanry Regiments - A pictorial history - P. J. R. Mileham, Spellmount, 1985

LMS Sectional Appendix (Northern Division) - March 1937, Author's collection

HR Weekly Notice 839 - June 1914, National Records of Scotland ref BR/HR/30/5

HR Station Opening/Closing Dates, Highland Railway Society, 1991

HR's *Official A.B.C. Tourist Guide, 1908*, Highland Railway Society collection

HR's Line widening contracts: Blair Atholl & (County March) Drumochter
  No.1 Struan Contract, No.2 Dalnaspidal Contract, 1898
  Non-specific *Contract Specification*, 1900.

I have also relied upon several Collections and Archives:

My own collection of photographs, documents and notes gathered over the years.

The Photograph Collection of the Highland Railway Society (HRS).

Books from the canon of Highland Railway history, too many to list here.

Newspapers of the time, e.g. *Perthshire Advertiser, Inverness Advertis*er.

National Census 1911; also 1861-1901 as transcribed by Ancestry.

Valuation Rolls for Blair Atholl 1885-1898.

Records at Scottish Record Office (now National Records of Scotland)
- BR/HR and BR/PDR series of Minutes, Letters, and other formal company records
- RHP series of plans and drawings

Parliamentary Acts (listed in *HR Acts Of Parliament* pub HRS 2003).

All illustrations marked 'GWW' are prints from original glass plates in the George Washington Wilson Collection which is held by the Special Collections Centre in the University Library, University of Aberdeen; all are reproduced by permission of the University of Aberdeen.

All the extracts from old Ordnance Maps are either from original sheets held by the Author or from the online resource of the Map Room of the National Library of Scotland; all are reproduced by permission of the Trustees of the National Library of Scotland.

All J L Stevenson photographs reproduced by permission of Hamish Stevenson.

Other illustrations acknowledged appropriately.

Cattle passing James Marshall's coal office along Goat Street into the goods yard to the railway loading bank. The station building is on the right - note the balcony around the rear; for the benefit of the Station Agent and his family, this emphasises its Swiss-Chalet aspirations. The Bowling Clubhouse is the thatched building in view. *(Atholl Country Life Museum)*

THE HIGHLAND RAILWAY SOCIETY

The Highland Railway Society caters for all those interested in the varied aspects of the railway, including its predecessors and its successors to the present day.

An illustrated quarterly *Journal* is distributed to members and contains a wide variety of articles and information. Members queries are a regular feature and details of new books, videos and models of interest are reported. An active Internet chat group stimulates discussion among members. The Society's publications include a series of books commemorating the 150th anniversaries of the opening of various sections of the system.

Meetings are held in both Scotland and England. An Annual Gathering is held each September and includes a full day of talks, films, etc., as well as an opportunity to meet fellow members.

The Society has Library, Photographic and Drawing collections which are available to members. Copies of drawings are available for purchase. Modellers are well catered for. Complete kits are produced in limited runs. Specially commissioned modelling components such as axle boxes, buffers and springs are available, plus a comprehensive set of transfers to enable any Highland loco to be named.

Membership details can be found on the our website at www.hrsoc.org.uk.

Taken in late LMS days with the layout now fully developed. (postcard author's collection)

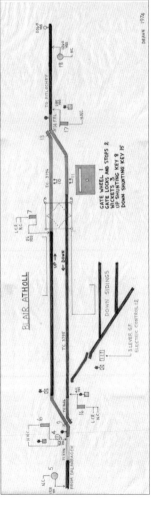

(Above) Signalling diagram for Blair Atholl in 1974, when the line north was single track. At most stations on the line, one track through the passing loop was arranged for fast running in both directions, but not at Blair Atholl. All trains had to slow when entering the loop. (HRS collection)
(Right) Many of the levers in the south signal box are now short ones, indicating that they operate motorised equipment or colour light signals. (Howard Geddes)